Lacuna Park

SPBH EDITIONS

Lacuna Park

Essays and Other Adventures in Photography

Nicholas Muellner

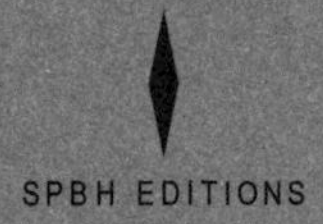

SPBH EDITIONS

Besides, consider the advantage of a vocation which necessitates one's being a taking woman.

—Gertrude Kasebier, *Studies in Photography*, 1898

A
Start

I BEGIN WITH THE OBVIOUS: we are all going to die, but we hope to *feel* a lot of things first. I begin with the obvious because for my purposes, a photograph is a surface for feeling.

Photography has never meant anything singular as a medium. To be sure, what we call photography has passed through an almost constantly shifting array of technologies that enable and obsolesce certain media forms. But these technologies and forms are transient. Photography is best understood across time as a set of relations, and a way of engaging: with oneself, with the world, and with others. A surface for feeling.

Traditionally, there has been a certain small subset of humans for whom using the technologies of photography amounted to a survival strategy, an intervention in their relationship to the world that allowed them to live in it. A therapist might call it a "compromise formation" – a structural compensation for a fear, a weakness, an insatiable desire. Such people are what I have long termed photographers – individuals for whom something existential is at stake in the making of photographs. I am one such desperate soul: a photographer.

Over the past decade, smartphones, and their fathomless portals for sent and posted images, have carved an ever-deepening chasm between each of us and the world we live in. As a perverse result, the ranks of those fitting my old definition of "the photographer" have recently swollen beyond rational count. Billions of people suddenly have something existential at stake in photography.

Photography was never a single medium, but it has always been an analogue – for being and feeling and the spaces between living and knowing. Image-making is experience and experience makes images. Analogues stand in for the original, the subject, but they also elucidate it; they make it readable in an economy of meaning. They intercede between us and the world on someone or something's behalf. They change our relation to the subject, even though they never seem to become it.

What is at stake in the making, using and viewing of photographs? This question, more than issues of form, technology, subject or style, is the one that keeps me going. It is a question of how we relate. How we control and care and lose and desire and most of all, how we adapt and compensate. How we learn and forget and remember and keep going. All of that happens through images.

The answers to this question have been shifting, expanding and contracting at an astonishing rate over the decade during which the words and images in this book were assembled. At times, my mind has felt like an insufficient focusing mechanism, straining to capture a herd of strange shapes, hurtling across a dark plain. This book attempts to track the moving target of what is at stake for photographers, which this year defines nearly all of us.

May, 2019

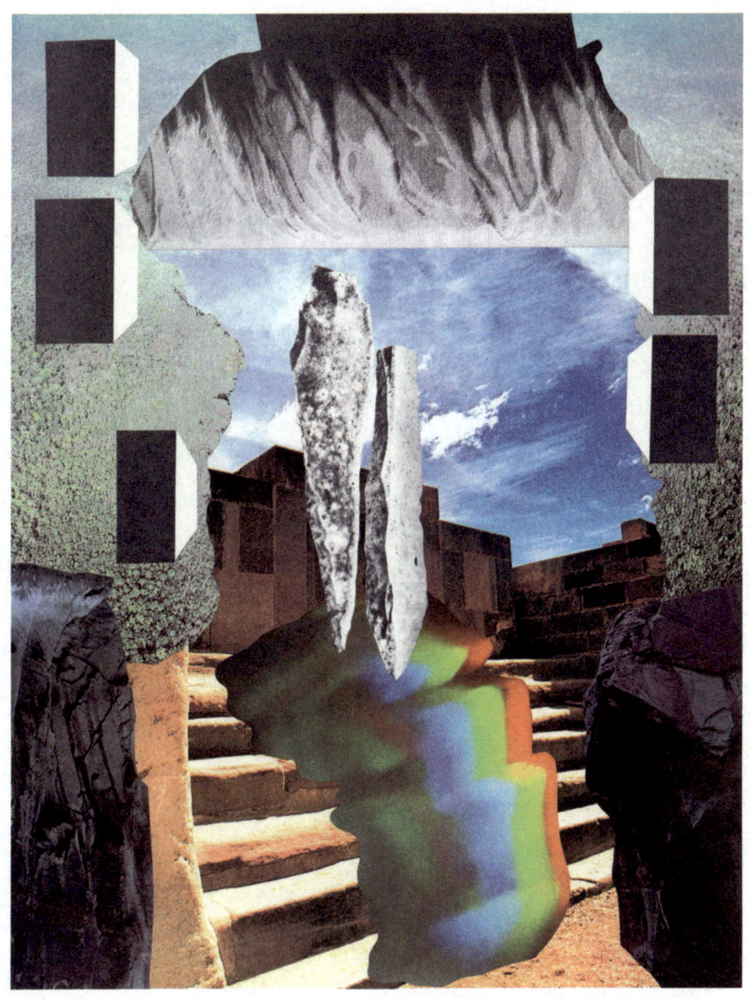

I.

Making Doubles

READER BEWARE. This essay has failed. I have been trying to build it for over a decade, but each new edifice of argument inevitably collapses in a contradictory heap of rubble. I have finally come to accept this essay as wreckage: the articulated ruins of an unfinished architecture. It's what I deserve for asking myself a trick question, for trying to build at a time when all the fault lines seem active. I wanted you to see what I have been feeling, but the ground kept shifting beneath my heart.

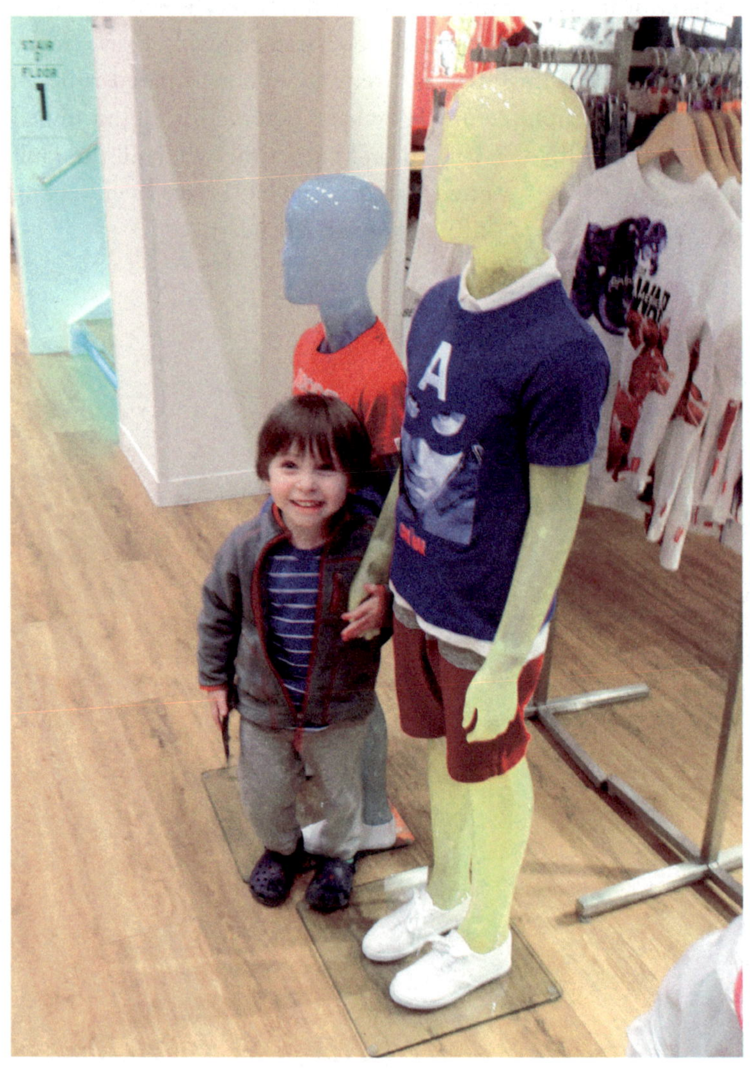

Episode 1

I can't stop looking at the picture, slightly blurry, forwarded from my sister's phone: My nephew, barely three years old, is beaming. Slightly too-long bangs brushed roughly away from his face, eyes engaging the camera, his left hand grips the larger, cooler hand of a Uniqlo store mannequin in a royal blue T-shirt. My nephew looks ecstatic, as if he has just made a new and lasting friend. But I also think, with a sigh: *He is learning.*

I'm sure that my brother-in-law, taking the picture, and my sister, just out of frame, do not see it this way. I'm sure I wouldn't have either, were I there, with my clever and adorable nephew. I'm sure I would have marveled at his giddy enjoyment of the scene, himself free from the obligation to shop, select and spend. His sensations and expressions would seem purely his own – my marvelous nephew, making his world as he makes sense of ours.

For all the delight of the photograph, I cannot escape the chill. A certainty of what he is being shaped into at that very moment. The invisible shadow of relentless economic and cultural systems closing in on him with their sparkly selections, their inanimate stand-ins taking him by the hand. In the picture, we can see, the coercion of capital is no joke. It is a web and a spectacle, and he is already entangled.

In person, the next time I see him, I learn all about the *Batman*-themed sneakers he wants, inspired by envy of another child. But hearing him tell it, I am reassured by his presence and spirit – it seems self-evident to me that his individuality will triumph over consumerist conformity. He loves Batman in his own way, I reason. His charming self is pure. But the photograph, arriving wirelessly to my remote device, had told me otherwise. Why was that?

What, I wonder, is the relationship between that delicious, terrible pedagogy we so often forget to call ideology, and our appearances in pictures? This question germinated for me in 2007, when

I was organizing an exhibition in Moscow about the common psychic and emotional experiences – expressed through contemporary art – of living in G.W. Bush-era America and Putin-era Russia. I had been trying to figure out why artists, and people in general, had such a hard time responding to the experience of living within the oppressions of coercive belief by saying *no*. Why was it so easy for us to recognize the condition, and then willingly collude? Why was it so difficult to refuse, withdraw or attempt change?

In the process of mulling over this conundrum, by no means a new one, I was suddenly struck by the old specter of Dostoevsky's *The Double*. As a teenager, I felt that Dostoevsky was all about angst and personal moral-emotional struggle. But I could not see that his work was also, always, about the pain of living in ideology. And the figure of the double, invented by his pathetic hero's unconscious as a desperate response to psychic pain, suddenly appeared to me as a figure we all share without knowing it: the double of ourselves that must navigate (successfully) within the logic of socioeconomic forces, so that we can pretend that we have a purer self, one outside of the systems of dogma and power that surround and shape us.

The tragedy of Dostoevsky's protagonist is that his double, happily navigating the mores and goals of his social circumstance, succeeds in all the ways that the original man cannot. His double is efficient and politic at work, effortlessly ambitious in society – a truly successful conformist in a way that the earnest, emotional clerk could never be. But purity of self has its cost. The double replaces him, and destroys his life.

His double annihilates him by successfully navigating the class cues of society: of capital and politics as rendered through social mores, fashion, and notions of production and consumption. As readers, we *hate* that double, for his inauthenticity, for his intentionality . . . but of course we fear that we are closer to the double than to that poor, hapless clerk. And we don't really want to end up like that loser anyway.

In Dostoevsky's novella, the double is clearly accepted as another – not the self but another self – and the one preferred by authority and society. The favored child of coercive learning. It is not an abstraction or a fantasy. The submitting double supplants the actual, stubborn self.

But what did this mean to me, exactly? And why was I convinced that photographs played a crucial role in this collective, and largely unacknowledged, psychic split? I did not know, and I was in Moscow, being physically pushed every day on the Metro by the sheer force of post-communist, high-capitalist frenzy. It was all I could do to remain upright; I put the question aside.

Episode 2

Nearly 20 years before my sister sent me that photograph of my nephew, a friend came in to work one day with a treasured family snapshot. It was the mid-1990s, when photography had finally become "Art," but nothing meant anything anyway, because history had ended, along with television and pop music. She gleefully shared the old photograph around the office, and everyone laughed, and loved it: My friend, as a child, stood proudly midframe, bare legs between short yellow shorts and stark white socks, a pastel-striped polo shirt leading the eye upwards to a white hat with a wide black visor. A look of sun-blasted seriousness compressed her face. Three smaller girls flanked her, two left and one right. And interspersed among them, a couple of Cabbage Patch dolls. All of them, including the dolls, had their arms stretched out, clasping other hands. It was Hands Across America — that absurdly momentous spectacle of 1986, attempting to forge an unbroken chain of humanity across the full breadth of Reagan's America. I did not trust my own memory, so I immediately wrote my friend, and she immediately sent me a copy of the image in question. It was almost exactly as I had remembered. There, in the middle of it, was Nikki. Holding hands with a Cabbage Patch Kid! In Hands Across America!

What made this image so hysterical? I think it was the shock of someone you know — an irreducible individual — suddenly flattened into the ideological spectacle of mass culture. As if Nikki was temporarily not Nikki: reduced before my eyes to a link in the chain of Hands Across America, a Cabbage Patch consumer. This transformation, of known soul and self into the raw stuff of collectively coerced belief (the social) had to be a laugh-riot. Because if it wasn't laughable, it was true! This is one true terror of the double — a terror made plain to us in the photograph, at

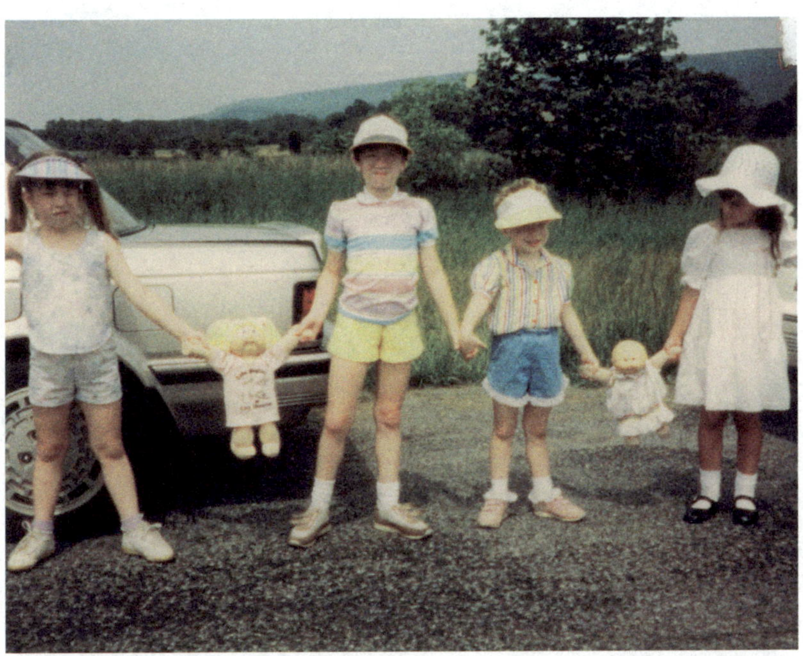

the same time as this truth is flattened, contained, bracketed safely away from the ultimate self.

But how does this dubious mechanism operate? Are we able to see ourselves as material subjects of power in photographs because we are flattened onto the same plane as any other given thing: chairs, walls, cups and countertops equally present and equally objectified? In life, objects seem to submit to the authority of our animate, willed selves. In the photograph, we are no more autonomous than the mass-produced T-shirt and jeans we are wearing, the store-bought lamp that illuminates us, the can of beer in our hands. It's a way of seeing what we can't perceive from inside our own bodies. The photograph maps our double's inevitably enmeshed status in the world of capital, and its junk materials of ideology.

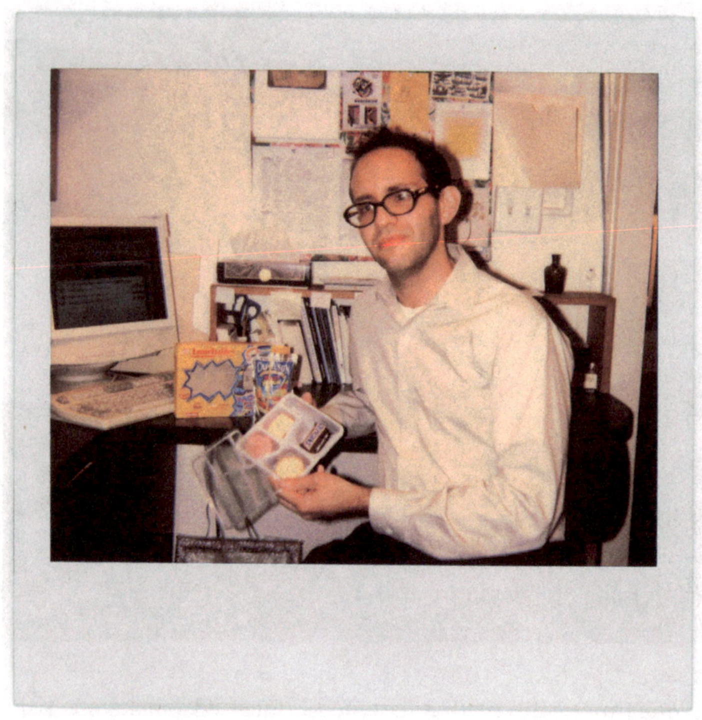

The author at work

To be only an object is a disappointment, and a gift. It is a kind of relief, and a comfort of belonging, to see oneself so clearly subsumed by the general condition of a culture. Are we let off the hook, as aspiring individuals, when we are reminded of this blind submission – freed from the need to define oneself, to forge an original self, to be distinct? Photographs don't steal your soul, but they might reveal quite bluntly that you are not one.

It was early in 2016 when I remembered Nikki's photograph, and already the air was thick with politics. Every hour, I read something new, to fill me with rage or hope or sadness. There was no room to finish a thought.

Episode 3

My next double-date was with Joseph Conrad's strange, dark, homoerotic short story, "The Secret Sharer." Conrad's narrator, a responsible, bourgeois ship's captain, meets and harbors his murderous double, enjoying their intimate seclusion in his private quarters while the law closes in around them. The captain then helps his homicidal duplicate escape into an island paradise, alone, naked, unpunished, while the captain, blameless but gratified, continues on the return journey to civilization.

Conrad's narrator discovers the erotic potential of the murderous self . . . but still submits to the necessity of living within society's bounds, by sending that unfettered, powerful, naked self away, and continuing on alone. The double transgresses on behalf of the self, but must also disappear. Still, the captain knows that his handsome, violent, uncontrolled double is out there, somewhere, beyond the laws. The double gets off scot-free.

I want to insist that the self, reproduced in the picture, is also an agent of possibility, like Conrad's murdering double. The photographer Luigi Ghirri writes:

> Photography is not mere duplication, nor is the camera simply an optical device that brings the physical world to a halt; photography is a language in which the difference between reproduction and interpretation, however subtle, exists and gives rise to an infinite number of imaginary worlds. Even the objects that seem to be entirely described by our own seeing, once represented may turn out to be like the blank pages of a book yet to be written.

And this unwritten book can be autobiography, by which I mean fiction. The you in the picture is never you. In becoming that double it both menaces and protects the self. It creates the space for transgressive or conformist fantasies. Ghirri suggests that in a photograph we can imagine a blank page where there isn't one. On the one hand, we can see our second self, subject to the cruel generality of culture, society, economy. This other us is trapped in the picture, while we float free.

But our duplicate can also be the image, like Conrad's double, that escapes the compromises of the social because it seems to confirm so intensely the singularity of a given self. Look at that expression, that smile, that set of jaw, that twinkling eye, that awkward or elegant carriage, that silhouette. Look, we tell each other, that image is a quintessence of you.

The photograph helps us enact a potentially perverse joy we take in dissolving into the manufactured collectivity of mass culture, while making a vain attempt to preserve "individuality" within that very act of collusion. Watching the Super Bowl, we are all the same, in that none of us matters. We are data points of an astonishing statistic of mass submission. In the car, inadvertently tapping our feet to an awful Bruno Mars ditty or a ravishing Beyoncé ballad, we are the same (the judgments there are mine; they do not matter). Why do we think that the image of ourselves in the teeth of this mass consumption, which feels so good precisely because it lets us feel part of a giant flood of collectively seduced humanity, somehow singles us out?

How do we belong without disappearing? How do we resist without disappearing? Are there two more impossible questions in the world?

Episode 4

I realize that I have been ignoring the central question of time, that great dog-wag of photography. So I decide to begin again, mindful that time, today, is not what it once was.

The future is always a blind curve in the road, but we don't see it, because we are usually looking down. In the photograph, we can recognize that the self is always frozen on the brink of the moment after. Something happens to us, seen in photographs, even if those images are only days or weeks old. Something that I can only call painful. We see ourselves in a state of frozen ignorance. That floating moment of us is necessarily unaware of everything that we are yet to encounter. It is a smiling, happy, confident blindness. But that momentary spectacle of us also seems to have lost or forgotten everything that came before it. To have offered itself up to a surface without history – born anew in naive confidence without knowing all the past that was carried in the four-dimensional original. There is nothing more freeing – and more vulnerable – than knowing neither past nor future. Pure presence is not something we are often able to live, but we can see it here, for better and for worse, when we are pictured.

But this last paragraph is already as out of date as an iPhone 4. These days, the present refreshes as fast as we can type. The present of the text that I just received has been replaced by the present in which I am typing my response. And the photograph seems to serve this god of the endless, tedious, anxious present more readily than the old gods of nostalgia and prognostication. We now willingly assign our images a 24-hour shelf life. After that, existence needs to be proven all over again. We offer our present up as a near-constant commodity for the use and profit of a distant corporate demigod. This is what I mean by tribute.

We are trying to tell each other, and ourselves, that we're alive and well, that we're happy, or sometimes sad, but always whole and "present" and looking our best. It is a strike against both past and future to treat an image that way. It denudes history and possibility at once, but who has time? We can always stream more history and possibility later, when we need it.

Is it possible that people take and circulate so many pictures these days not because they can, but because, for existential reasons, they have to? Perhaps the more time they spend with their primary attention dedicated to a technological product that is itself a portal into endless forms of "free" consumption – products, politics and every kind of social conditioning – the more they need to reaffirm their individual existence, or sacrifice an image of themselves to the indifferent gods of sociocultural submission, in the name of their imperiled identities. That is no longer a question of future or past, of hope or memory. It is a constantly refreshing existential crisis.

Our skin in an image, from messaging to Tinder to Grindr, is often used as a kind of virtual bait. We dangle a trace of ourselves, deployed to lead our quarry – the objects from whom we desire attention – back to our actual lives. Our image is now a "link" or "tag" to our physical manifestation. A link is not a representation, a memory or an imagining. It is an instrument, an icon, a reminder, a reference. It may also be our last hope, telegraphing our ongoing desire to be touched.

Perhaps all of this explains why, when I look at a selfie, I smell fear. Such a banal synesthesia, I know. I can't help but sense the act as an anxiety response – people reassuring themselves that they're still there; reminding others that they exist. That they can still surrender themselves to the camera. I recall someone telling me: "You should really post on Instagram at least three times a day, lest you fall off the map."

I ask myself, writing this essay, why I keep referring, absurdly, to old gods and new gods when I don't believe in gods. I think it's because I am weak and need metaphors, and a pagan theology makes sense in the world we live in. Our gods of society, politics and capital place competing demands on the individual, and each other. There is a complex economy of ritual, sacrifice and reward that has none of the clear, hierarchical organization of those more ridiculous monotheisms. Nobody suffered in advance for our sins; this system is pay as you go. The gods care not for our souls, but only for their agendas. The god *techne* gave us photography and she expects a reward. Our pictures are our currency; we return them like burnt offerings.

Episode 5

Now, as I write, it is one endless week before the 2016 Election Day. This whole, grinding, pervasive, painful, emotional, hopeful, tragic election cycle has drawn on so long, and taken so much out of us. I feel myself in pain at the suffering that the ideological, in one of its most melodramatic incarnations, has wrought so directly, readably, on our lives, to so many degrees, in so many registers, with such a range of bodily and immaterial consequences. How could we not want *something* to make us feel free of it? Under this dark fog, I have found myself looking over and over at pictures of myself and others, drawn to the innocence of the figure not registering their placement within coercive learning. A hopeful gleam ignorantly flashing forth a signal of imagined freedom; not an escape, but a willing – and unaware – submission. This gesture lives on in the photograph, without consequence, repercussion, blame or regret. Such photographs promise to lift the burden off me, over and over again, and always only for the moment of exchange.

In 1859, Oliver Wendell Holmes erroneously predicted the replacement of most touristic travel with the advent of great stereographic libraries in every city. Citizens of all stations would enjoy the three-dimensional illusion produced by a doubled photograph inserted in an optical viewing device and feel themselves transported to Paris, Petra, the Taj Mahal or an African safari. Holmes asserted that photographed subjects, like big game, surrendered up their skins, to be picked up by the film plane and carried away for all to see. These "skins" (spoken in the colonialist argot of the hunting trophy) were ill-defined, but they seemed to be inexhaustible, and every single *thing* on earth had many skins to spare.

It is as if we "individuals" think that our own skins can be similarly shed, in photographic sacrifice, over and over again – carrying away our sullied surfaces that are exposed to all manner of social coercion and leaving our pure interior souls intact.

The categories of the "individual" and "humanity" are brilliantly and cruelly designed to occlude ideological systems. This is obvious; in fact, it is an Althusserian (and 1960s Godardian) Obviousness. But the role of the photograph has not been fully understood in this regard. It is not only a medium of indoctrination, it is also a release valve and an illusionary removal system. Like Silly Putty on a newspaper comic. The image of ourselves trapped within markets and social and political coercions is, over and over again, lifted away from us in a photograph. A kind of facial peel for the spiritually imperiled self.

Episode 6

Perhaps I've been approaching this wrong, it occurs to me, a week after the election. Now, it no longer feels like photographs can carry anything for us. The image of a hideous man spouting a seeming incoherency of violent, cruel, petulant and occasionally sensible assertions has "won" power. We are passing over into one of those societies in which the exercise of ideology is unavoidably material, physical and visible — a manifest violence. Suddenly, we have become our aloof doubles, and the reality is not what we had imagined. It hurts and it menaces. The illusion of distance that neoliberalism has allowed seems, all the sudden, quaint. As if it had no intention or fault in taking us here.

We no longer have use for the suspension of the free self in the ether of the remotely ideological. We are now in the world of video clips: beatings, mobs, speeches, massing, fluid shows of force, aerial views of scattering resistance, roundups, lines, threats, deportations. Photography is inadequate to these events. The double, and the cushion of plausible difference it sustained, feels suddenly, utterly, gone.

But are we moved to step away from the photograph here, taking up the yoke of the political, without need or possibility of release? Mostly, the answer is no. Instead, we double down on images with a will to see ourselves and be seen within the immediately identifiable struggle. Protest-march selfies abound, as do panning videos that assert the photographer at the center of a mobilized citizenry. For a moment, we are *in it*, our images insist. But then we are not. We let the photograph stand before us, as a placeholder of our embeddedness, while we slink back to our jobs, our joys, our personal struggles, as if our doubles will carry on the fight for us.

I still remember the pride — or perhaps relief — that my parents exuded when they would stop on a photograph of my father —

young and beautiful, my older brother on his shoulders – marching against the Vietnam War on the Washington Mall in 1969. My parents have never been activists, but this one image lived as a promissory tableau of their impassioned participation. A proof that they were in the fight, even as they left or never really joined. I do not blame them; they had four children. I have a dog and I have done no better.

Sometimes we desperately need to see ourselves within the dastardly machine of coercive belief, for reasons of survival, to advance our desires and ideals in the world, or to provide the illusion of power that belonging implies. Photographs can carry that embrace or submission for us.

Once, at a flea market in Rome, I came across three black-and-white photographs dated 1938. In each image, two young men from Fascist Italy pose in front of the landmarks of Fascist Berlin. The men are perhaps in their early thirties – they are relatively small in the frame, their faces shaded by their fedoras, their bodies lost under long overcoats – and they appear focused in posture, gaze and set of jaw. The serious place at which tourism and pilgrimage meet. There they stand, in naive pride, before the swastika-draped Reichstag. Their doubles, here, testify for posterity to their accord with the terrible splendor of what we now, so casually (too casually – as it if it is OK!) call nationalism. I had the sensation that if I held the thin prints up to the light in the right way, these words would appear: *I am white. Help me stay that way.*

<u>Episode 7</u>

More than a year into this terrible government, this mean and messy presidency, I am thinking about the double again. And I find that all the above arguments feel moot. What made me think that a photograph rescued or killed anything? At most it was a thin piece of paper, now a density of dots on a screen for a moment that is instantly replaced by another.

In Dostoevsky's imagining — a world in which the paranoid becomes true — the double annihilates and replaces the original. The irreducible self is gone. Are all these images simply the equivalent of a hospital modesty screen, helping our neighbors not to witness the death throes of our original souls.

We all want a politics that leaves room for the self, but that might be too much to ask. To live consciously and aware within ideology (writ large as the social, or writ small as politics) is hard, because the mechanism is so rigged, and it can feel impossible to trace or remedy how we got here. Magic tricks are supposed to be thrilling, but this trick is awful.

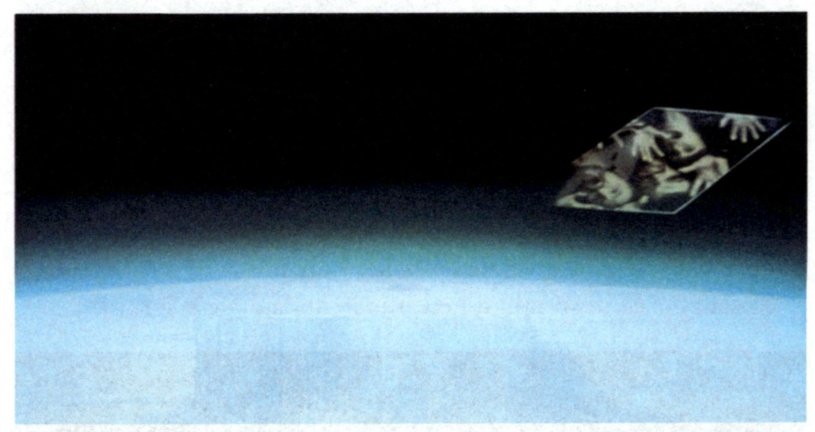

Episode 8

I want to go back and start over, this time in 1980.

Superman II, starring Christopher Reeve, begins with the trial of Krypton's traitors, who resemble nothing so much as a new-wave-inflected European post-punk pop band. For their treachery, the band is banished in a most dramatic way: flattened, alive, into a two-dimensional rectangular plane, which flies in to claim them, and then spins out again into the void of space. General Zod and his coconspirators scream in helpless rage, six mime-hands splayed desperately against the clear surface of their new jail. Of course, our own fate with photographs is less dire than this, as we seem to continue on just fine while our image remains in the flattened plane. Nonetheless, photographs are prisons, trapping us in the moral judgment of the will of law, which is sometimes called the social contract. Photographs lock up the crime – the submission, the collusion – but not the criminal, whom we may also call the victim, the hero or the bystander.

In Philadelphia, in the early 1990s, I worked as an in-house photographer for a corrupt and sadistic art dealer. In those days, "making doubles" was something you did whenever you were getting prints made and might want to share them with friends or family (or send images of overpriced inventory to unsuspecting clients). Making doubles was a minor investment in the pre-digital image-sharing economy. And since the printing was on my boss's account, I made doubles of everything, as a kind of tax on my employee suffering. Thousands of doubles that piled up, untouched. This whole episode of my life still lives in duplicate, in boxes, in an unfinished attic in upstate New York.

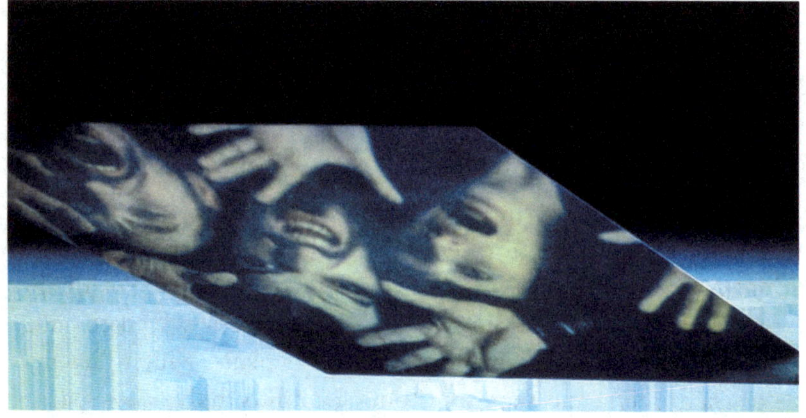

Today, the concept of doubles, or any multiples of images, is nearly moot. The image is both singular – a specific file with a specific arrangement of pixels – and infinite. It is no longer "reproduced." When you upload an image, it also stays where it was; when you download an image, it does not seem to notice.

Perhaps, within that new ontology of photographs – always there and always singular – it is now easier to believe that you are singularly represented by an image that nonetheless proliferates – is available – almost anywhere. There are no longer any copies.

In some senses, this is a mercy. I recently unearthed a stack of these doubles that I had made in the art gallery. In each photograph, the object – an antique map, rare book or decorative print – was duly displayed against black fabric and elegantly, evenly lit. But approaching clumsily from the side, with an unfortunate early 1990s goatee and round silver spectacles, was me, staring straight at the lens, as if I also expected to be a rare commodity. The objects kept changing, but my dress and place and gaze did not alter.

I cannot even remotely recall the impulse that made me take these pictures. But the effect of this doubled me – asserting over and over again some unknown argument for my own presence, identically, twice – was almost unbearable to look at. The value and rarity of the objects that accompanied me may have been exaggerated or overestimated, but this double me was certainly false – not even a man: two tediously identical reproductions, each obliterating the authenticity of the other.

Photographs have a way of humiliating the original.

Why does it seem so hard to be "ourselves" in ideology? Or, to put it another way, where did we get the idea that our true selves are more than the sum of our movement through the indoctrinations of the social? Of course, it is society that supplied the idea of our individual authenticities in the first place. Even recognizing that, it is a hard idea to give up on. Ask Walter Benjamin, that committed Marxist. He could never get over himself.

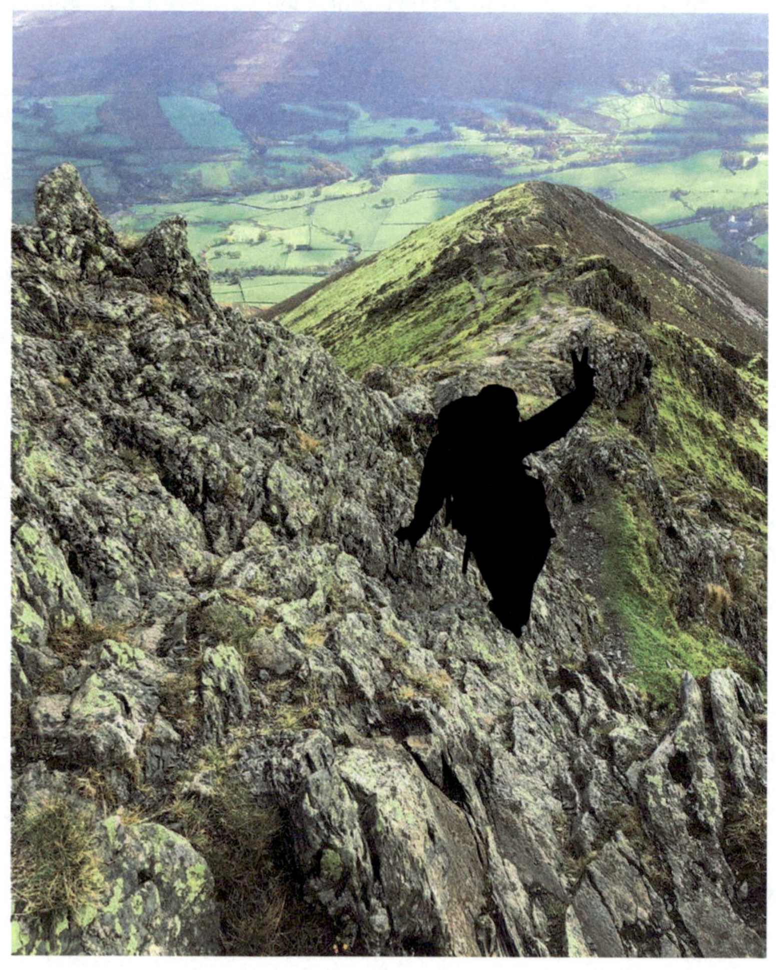

Episode 9

To most people, I must assume, the self on the screen feels continuous with their daily, lived self. It may even serve to affirm to them their authenticity. Maybe these pictures say: *Just me being me!*

Your friend posts a selfie. She is red-faced with triumphant exertion, standing atop a mountain with a scenic vista behind her. She is smiling vigorously, and flashing the peace sign with her free hand. You might look at the image and know her well enough to understand that she does not subscribe to the banal intellectual collapse that peace sign layered over beautiful nature implies. She is not a peddler of this contemptible hippie solecism equating naive pacifism with a love of the great outdoors, most useful to the political right as a means to dismiss serious ecological concerns. She is well informed on global warming; she is conscientious, environmentally aware, and she votes. But there she is. And you forgive her automatically; you laugh. You might have done the same. Because, in this overwhelming world, flattening — of the complexity of ideas, of your body against vast nature, or your far away friend into the near space of your heart — is such a relief. Thank god we have these doubles to do it for us.

Your friend might also instinctively already understand that posting a picture is akin to asking a question of a strange Magic 8 Ball, where the answer, algorithmically conjured, always comes back as one word: *submit.* Contextualized as these images are within the indexing and identity-crafting structures of social media, there is no outside of conformity. We are either conforming forthrightly to one idea of self, or conforming to non-conformity. In this space, they are the same thing.

Sabrina Harman, one of the young soldier-photographers at Abu Ghraib, posed before dead and tortured bodies with a broad smile and an enthusiastic thumbs-up. She claimed to have taken the pictures to document what she knew to be criminal, but the world countered: *You look so happy!* I think she understood more about the double than the rest of us. She knew, on some level, that she was serving up as sacrifice an image of herself, enacting collusion with the violence of power in the readable tableau of the flat photograph, to show us that something was wrong. She sent her double-agent into the world to shock us into shame.

Perhaps we unconsciously offer up our inauthentic selves, flattened into caricatures of social submission, to secretly inform the future that these doubles are not really us? A coded message transmitted by us hostages: *Something is terribly wrong.*

Episode 10

Ever since the 2016 election, I have wanted to photograph the world, and especially individuals, only as refracted in mirrors. The mirror is not a photograph – a reflection is not a double – and you can see that in these pictures. In the glass, we encounter our image on equal footing. We arrive and depart together; we continue to breathe and blink in synchrony. My reflection and I are coextensive, and we seem to see each other. The reflection is our self; the photo is a double. When I go out, the mirror returns to being a picture of an empty room. I wonder if Jewish custom shrouds mirrors during mourning so we are not reminded too vigorously that our own lives continue. Mirrors restore me to my ongoing present. These days, mirrors make me feel a little better.

Some days, by the time I tap out of the album on my phone, I feel like I've just visited a prison of my exiled selves, floating in a limbo of still-pending judgments (was I happy, was I wise, was I honest, could I have been better?). I wish I could tell them all what I know now about the minutes, days and years around the curve in front of them; to lighten the load or help them bear it better. I close the album and continue with my day, while they hang there flattened, in weightless space, like so many *Superman* villains, plotting their revenge.

II.

Color
Correction

IN PHOTOGRAPHY, the preparation of color images for distribution involves a process prejudicially known as "color correction." Any overlying tonal cast is identified and removed so as to reveal the fullest range of "true" color in the image. It is a generally satisfying process, as a result of which objects appear purified, and the illusion of spatial depth enhanced. Affect is effaced in the service of accuracy.

Color correction assures the discrete separation of objects in an imaginary continuum of space. The serial solitude of perspective is enabled, relational collapse avoided. Everything gets to be alone in the same rectangular room.

The fundamental discourse of color correction runs along a warm-cold axis. In the neutralizing paradigm of the representational process, images are either too warm or too cool, too red (magenta and yellow) or too cyan (blue and green). Such excesses are easily rectified. Sometimes, though, the problem is not so easily identified. I have come to consider a certain subset of these troubled pictures to be bruised. They are suffused with a kind of underlying purple, at once too warm and too cool. Of course, there is a rational explanation for this state: too much magenta, and an excess of blue. But the answer takes me by surprise every time, because this imbalance always strikes me as a condition, rather than a fault. It materializes as a state in which affect hemorrhages from highlight into shadow, bleeding from sky into brooding foliage and across emotive expanses of dirt. Sometimes, the imbalance of the world (of the bruise) feels like this. The blue chill of distance and the magenta hue of desire comingle, opposite humors bleeding together beneath the picture's skin. This purple confuses depth, compromising the judicious extraction of one thing from another that constitutes our notions of seeing. Must this muddying always be remedied? Isn't this bruising also true?

Clean color lets us know that we are separate, that we are free. Is that absence of hue what we desire?

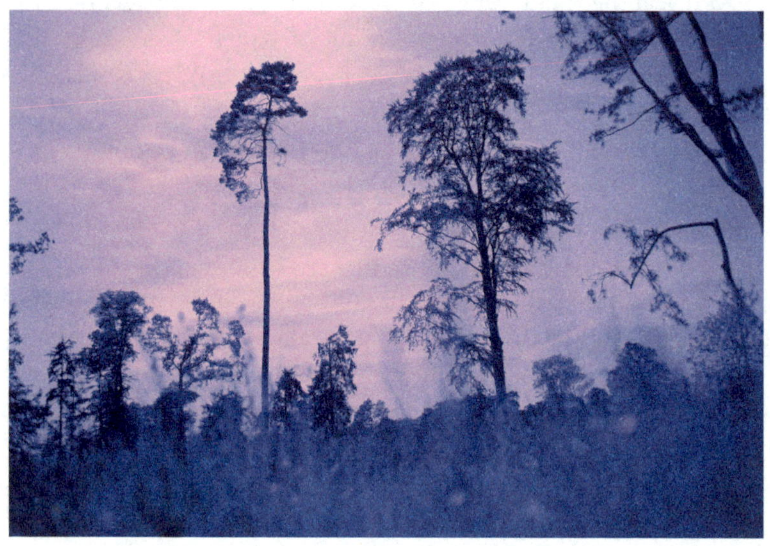

<u>I.</u>

Standing before me as I pause in the museum, Caspar David Friedrich's subjects turn their backs to me, unfathomable and– I always assume – uncomprehending before the distant confusion of the horizon. They are flattened against the painting's flatness, and between those two depthless notions – their minds, that vista – we find ourselves in unexpected suspense.

Friedrich's couples stare off together, delicately touching (hand on hand, hand on shoulder) while they share in the mystery of the distance. Side by side, they are united by the vanishing point, inviting us, too, as equals into the relationship. None of us look each other in the eye, even as my gaze flies past them into the deep space of the picture plane, pursuing the unreachable subject of their vision. Perversely, before Friedrich's foreclosures, I feel included. We are ignorant together, sharing one impossible horizon.

Friedrich's images, so often charged with the transitional dramas of dawn or dusk, are often bruised. Colors bleed, and the discrete laminates of the world's objects – humans, mountains, oceans, harbors, ruins, laid out in the vastness of space – become confused. How far are we from Friedrich's seekers? How far are they from their distant objects? The distance is both infinite and non-existent. Not atmospheric perspective, but an atmosphere without perspective.

In the commingling of refusal with sympathy that these paintings produce, a question brews: What is alienation and what is intimacy? Friedrich's answer arrives, over and over again, as an unorthodox equation: *Your distance makes me feel close to you.*

When we cannot penetrate the consciousness of the other, perhaps the space between individual and universe disappears, or wraps around us. We dissolve into the saturation of the sunset. Friedrich wants the space of eternity and the no-space of the picture plane to collapse on one another, because the force of that flattening leaves a mark. Like love, that beautiful mark might hurt.

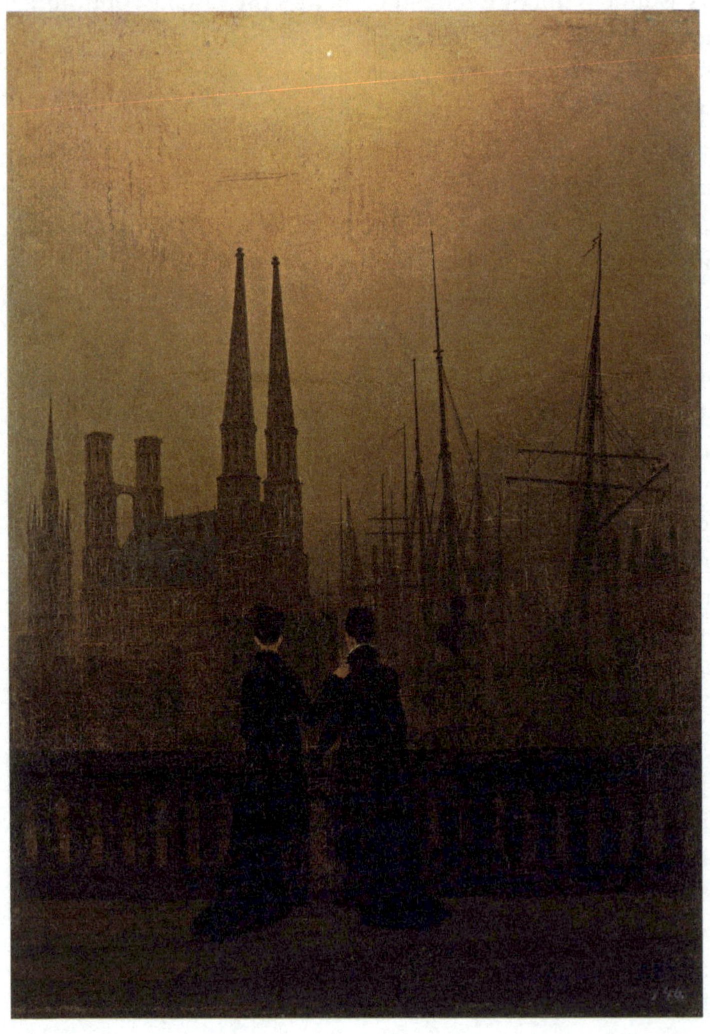

II.

We walk among the vast ruins, tracing individual paths that intersect, run parallel, draw apart. We drift but remain in orbit. We have only met yesterday, and we speak sparingly, the silence meaning both, "I don't know you at all," and, "What is there left to explain?" In these ruins, it seems we are joined by the hulking silence of the past, its distance much greater than that between us, and its presence, its palpability, much sounder than our own. I can't adequately explain why I wanted to meet Dima, and he doesn't even attempt to explain his own motives. It is, on both sides, a gesture stripped of practical intention, outside of desire, money, or even a conventional idea of friendship. Most likely, we will never meet again. I know only that, like a true Romantic, he has renounced the possibility of love.

In our correspondence, weeks before, I mentioned that I was a photographer. Dima answered, immediately: "Oh, then! We will have a lot to talk about!" But we didn't so much talk about photography as show photographs in place of talking. Sitting on the cramped bus, side by side, he pulled his tablet out of its leatherette sleeve. He then scrolled through his life, beginning from a recent hike and moving backwards through his last visit home, to the family farm in a Moldovan village, where each house makes its own wine. Dima on a hilltop; Dima by the lake; Dima with his mama; Dima holding grapes. His biography ended where his tablet began: a pastoral idyll signifying origins, family, happiness, nature. It told me nothing of his daily life as a café waiter, or about the one man he moved to Crimea to meet, from thousands of miles away, and who eventually threw him over. The tablet bore, instead, a silent mythos of the self he could still be: the vistas and memories that made him, enduringly, silently, only that Dima among so many.

Dima led me up a steep dirt path, past ancient stone turrets supported by haphazard wooden struts, to the natural ramparts that separate the Black Sea from the sheltered harbor below. Behind me, to the north, cast in fresh blue shadow, an empty tourist town clung to its placid waters, where centuries of alien armies have fortified themselves against local forces. In the west, the sun glowed yellow between two peaks. Dima and I, in silent agreement, moved away from each other, to contemplate the day's last dramas alone. My companion clambered onto the outermost cliff-top promontory, kneeling in silhouette against the desaturating aquamarine of the ocean. He looked south over the suddenly purple water, eyes squinting hard as if sufficient effort would discover Turkey. After a while, his head dropped down to contemplate the infinitesimal waves hitting sheer rocks hundreds of feet below. Eventually, he rocked back gently on his ass, tucking in his chin to take in his phone, glowing acid blue in the space between his knees.

I stood upon my own small promontory, contemplating Dima and the west as everything around us grew dark. In my overladen state, each of his gestures seemed to issue its own communiqué. Squinting at the horizon: a question of the future. Contemplating the surf below: the offering of death. Looking at his phone: Am I utterly alone? They probably said none of those things. But I have seen too many pictures, and I no longer know better. The image of the gaze is often a question of destiny, an imaginary refraction of fate beyond words. I turned away to stare eastward, where the high cliffs folded in on themselves densely, foreclosing contemplation. My body shielding the late sun from my camera's screen, I reviewed the photographs of Dima and the infinite I had just made — light, shadow, form and gesture extrapolated from the tableaux of moments ago. Already, his meaning was inscrutable. Despite the scale of the site, the light's tenderness eroded distance. The scene was intimate, internal, and not for me. My screen revealed merely what I saw: rock and sea and sun and Dima, together on a flat surface, conspiring to signal something to an interpreter unknown.

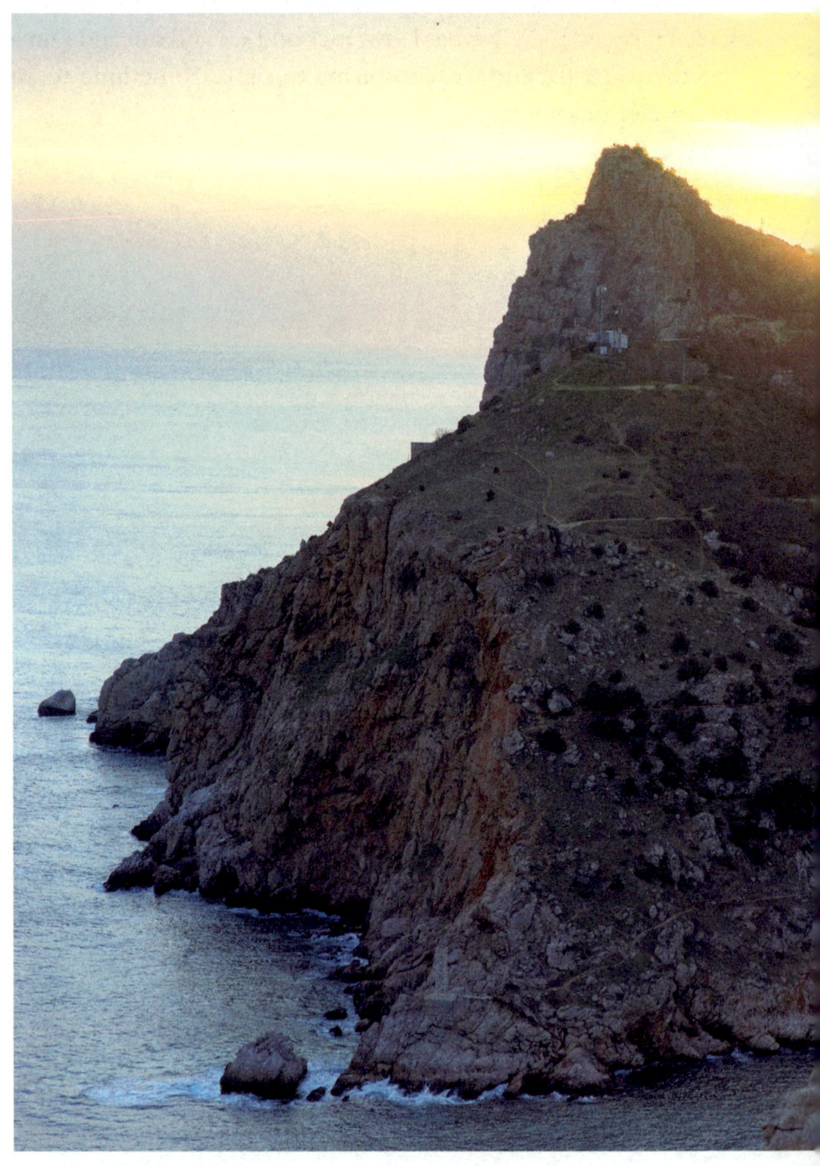

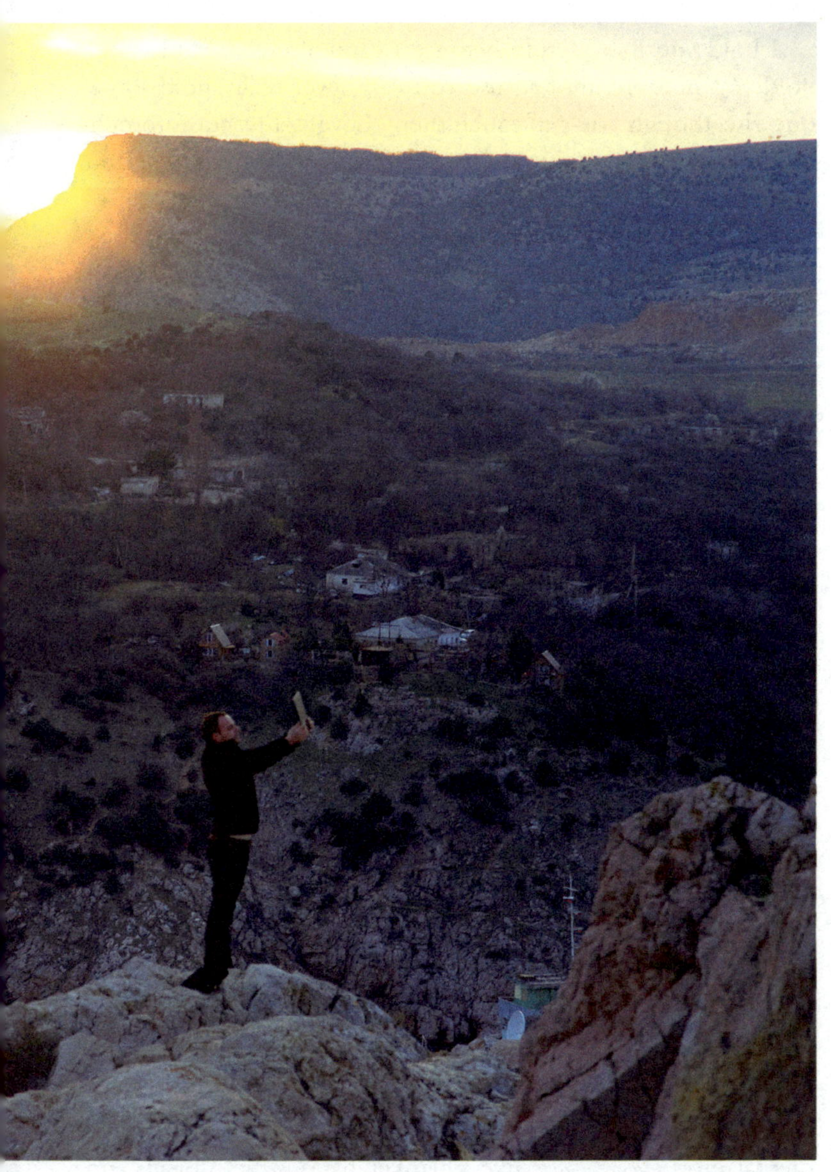

III.

I hold you in a picture because I cannot always hold you. I hold you in a picture because you can never really hold someone else, though you can touch them. Love is a reaction to radical distance. It is a reaching across, a drawing in from the horizon, more than an act of capture.

I like to imagine the Romantic space of Mark Morrisroe's world, which was unfolding in Boston in the early 1980s in all of its erotic, creative, marginal and vulnerable intensity, while I languished in the lonely, sexless, middle-class safety of my early-teen solitude just a couple miles away, as unaware of him as I was of myself.

Morrisroe is one of those artists whose lives seem impossible to separate from their work, because his experience, as well as himself, his homes, his friends and lovers, are always present in the frame. Thus, it seems wrong to distinguish the objects of his art from the actions of his life. I always feel the specters of his troubled youth and the cruelty of his death from AIDS, at 30, casting light from two directions across the fragile, ravaged paper of each print. The layered warmth of his comingling colors seems born of this unavoidable narrative. The print is less an image than an amber to preserve the love and lush confusion of youth lived boldly. Each image, a luminous suspension, protecting this tender life from the pain of the past and the murderousness of the future.

Morrisroe's prints bear the rough marks of their making, as if they had been held too long and too hard out of love. For all of their stains, marks, damage and discoloration – for all of their spectacular wrongness – they are among the most compelling images of caring I have ever seen. Their bruised colors, their fades, their chemical and manual saturations of unnatural tone, in overlays of yellow and blue and brown, suffuse the atmosphere with a sentimental, erotic fog. Color, like a blanket, flattens the subjects and their intimate spaces – bodies, beds, cats, bathtubs, framed pictures, blankets, bottles – into one inseparable fabric of shared warmth. Beneath these laminates of tone, they are all, always, touching each other, feeling one another's pain and love and vulnerable young skin. Color correction could only do violence to this tenderness. This intimacy demands that one thing bleed into the other. Youth has no space for perspective. And neither does dying.

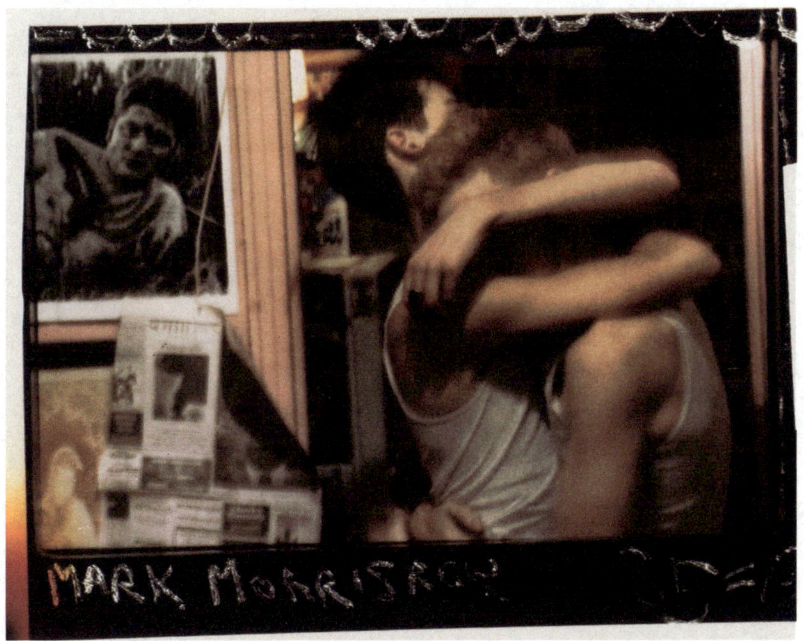

III.

A Minor Avant-Garde

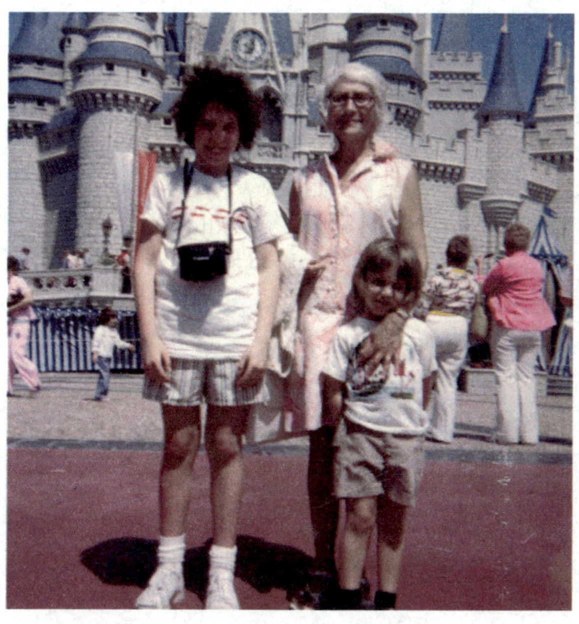

YOU CAN'T SEE MY TINY HANDS. They are clasped behind my back, eyes squinting into the Florida sun as I wait for my grandfather, possibly the worst photographer who ever lived, to memorialize this journey with his Instamatic. I am four years old, and already looking winsome. My older brother is 10, with his fancy new camera on a too-short strap around his neck, like a cowbell. He looks excited. We are about to enter Disney World for the first time, and he is tall enough for all the rides. My grandma Bea, very thin and almost always cold, stands in a sundress with a provisional sweater draped over her right arm. With her left, she clutches me protectively to her body. She looks, if not happy, at least proud. She also looks a little afraid – her pride is that of the soldier before battle; pride at her ready defense against the enemy. This is, after all, a photograph. And she stands before the diabolical gates of Disney.

Being loved by Grandma Bea had a special force behind it, because it was pretty clear that she didn't love much. She didn't enjoy eating or drinking or cooking; she hated visiting and hosting; she didn't like to travel. She mistrusted non-Jews, and disliked Jews who trusted in God or even pointed towards God through ritual. It was unclear how she loved her husband or her three desirous daughters. She liked Angie Dickinson in *Police Woman* and Raymond Burr in *Ironside*; she loved her grandchildren; and she hated photographs.

Or perhaps I should say that she took photographs seriously enough to fear them, and the likenesses they created. The pictures in her photo albums, and even in framed prints on walls or furniture, were punctuated with holes: jagged, hand-cut absences where heads had once been. Occasionally, these headless bodies belonged to relatives. Grandma Bea always claimed that she removed these faces because the subject had not looked good in the picture – that the removal was an act of courtesy towards their vanity. Because Grandma Bea was known to harbor grudges, one always suspected those decapitations had other agendas. But most of the removed heads were her own: She sliced out her own visage over and over again, rather than, say, not putting the picture in the album or on the side table. It was as if she wanted that gesture of violent self-removal to be evident, though she would never admit it.

I used to assume that this radical act was spurred by vanity. But I could not have been more wrong. Her cutting-out was no less than a strike against the materiality of her existence, reiterated through its duplication in the image. She hated her own objecthood, which photography made inescapable. She did not care for her appearance; she did not accept having appetites. Whenever she came to visit us, she would bring one or two items from her home that she simply could not bear to live with anymore: a plate, a single spoon. In her kitchen, she constantly decanted less-than-full containers into smaller ones, so as to minimize their presence. Even the milk, after a day's use, was poured from the carton into a smaller jar.

In the end, though she suffered from an obscure and slow-moving tuberculosis (rare in humans because the bacterium generally lives only in dirt), the disease did not kill her. Grandma Bea simply stopped eating. One of the last things I ever heard her say was, "I'm disillusioned with ice cream." And then she disappeared, finally achieving full excision.

My mother's mother did not appreciate the universe of things. The spectacle of consumerism, of participatory sociality, did not appeal to her. She clutched me to her body before the camera and the gates of Disney because in that moment, in that impending submission, we were, to her, imperiled.

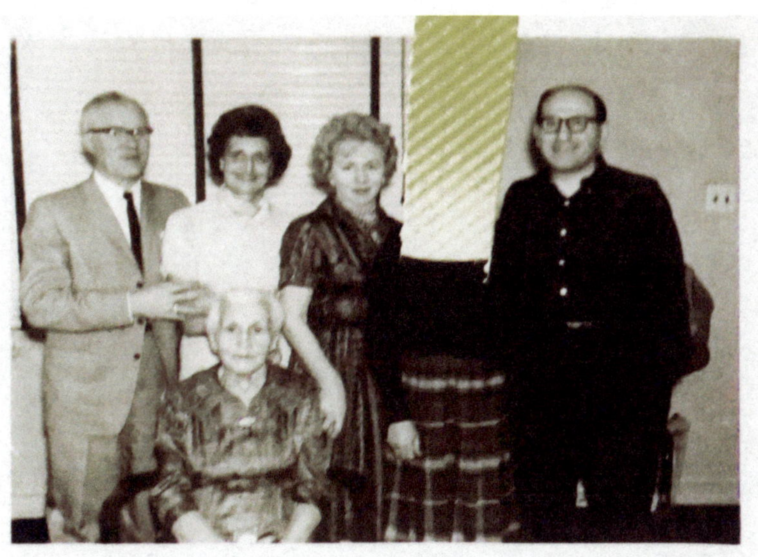

IV.

A Tug in Lisbon

A fiction for the photographs of
Gregory Halpern & Ahndraya Parlato

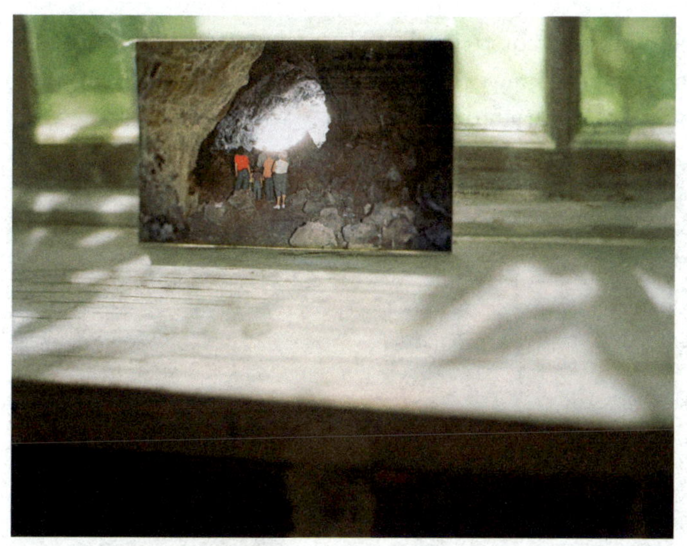

"TRANSIT," the Astronomer said, pausing for effect. "The word, as applied to humans, proposes a determinist pursuit: getting from one place to another. But the heavenly bodies, in their greater wisdom, have nowhere to go except around, or outward, and certainly no place to get to and stop. For them, content with perpetual rotation and drift, transit means something else: the crossing of one thing in front of another. It is no more or less than the alignment of bodies, without prejudice of purpose. Transit means the momentary coincidence of two trajectories — a sudden possibility that gives brief poetry to entropy's indifference. Afterwards, as before, the bodies are again moving outward, along, around, until further alignment occurs. Remember this," the Astronomer winked, "moving forward."

Imagine there were twins, who conspired in the womb to build a web between them. Pulled into the world, they arrived entangled in a filigree of threads, connecting their infant heads, back to back, in a neural cloud of shared sensation. Together from the beginning, they could see all angles at once. The twins missed nothing; they could never be taken by surprise. They could see everything save for each other.

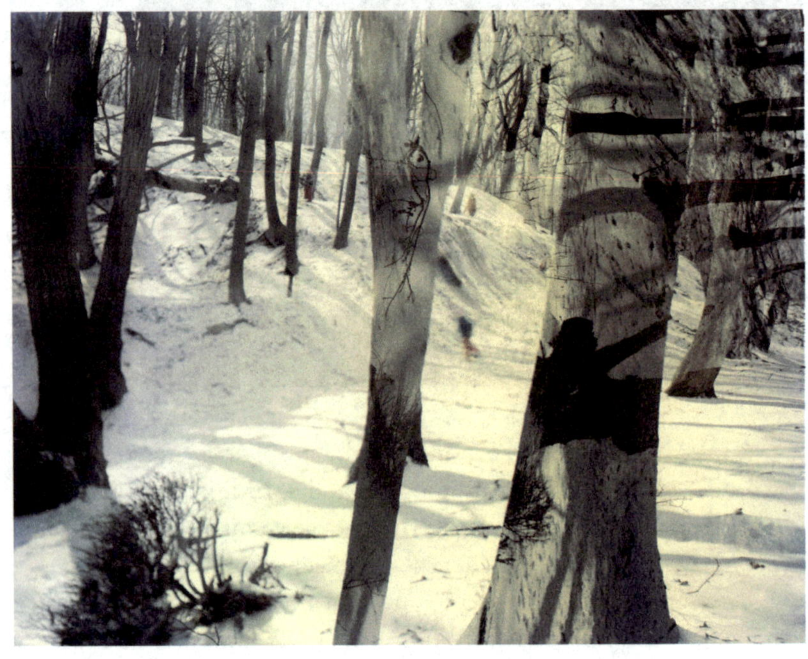

Eventually, the twins' guardians (there were no parents – this is not, after all, a psychological story), affronted by the toddlers' exclusive entanglement, had them trimmed and separated. Experts insisted they be sent as far from each other as possible to ensure their autonomous adjustment to our expectations of solitude. And so they were shipped apart, distanced by oceans and continents, and raised alone in alien lands, as close to absolute antipodes as the experts' web of contacts would allow. The westward twin grew up in Lisbon, the easterly twin in Melbourne. We will call them "Boa" and "Bourne."

Separated, their original web remained as only a feeling – abstract and gravitational in the most elusive of ways. Both suffered sensations that made the land unstable and the intentions of others obscure, as if each twin, alone, were not obeying the same forces as everyone else.

The twins grew up alleged natives in their respective cities, but neither felt settled in place. In Lisbon, Boa was addled by the dull howl of history – a sound like that of an old man sucking on the abscess of his lost tooth. Bourne was similarly nagged by the rustling of Melbourne's weightless past, its dry scrub rattling across the broad avenues at dawn. For the unknowing twins, history's accretion and its absence sounded very much the same: a broadcast of sourceless sounds by which neither one could navigate.

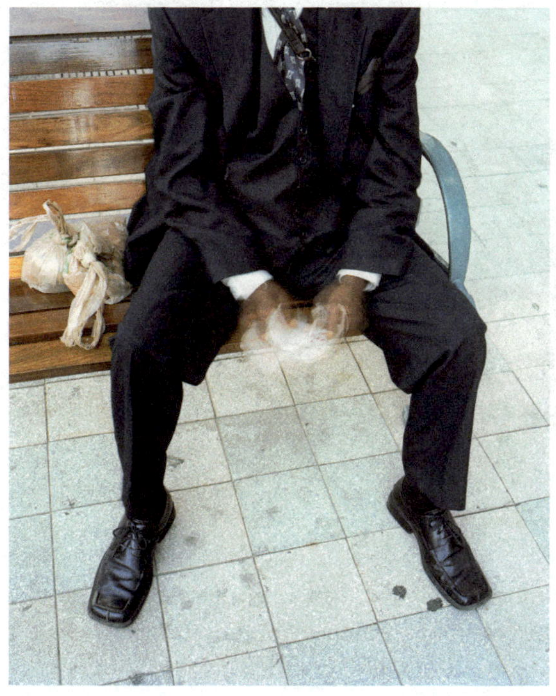

One bright winter day, Boa, unmoored and adult, had a strange sensation. This lost twin felt *tugged*. The pull was northward, inland, as if consciousness had been channeled like a wheel into one of Lisbon's infinite trolley tracks. Boa, thrilled to be oriented, obeyed.

For the first time, Boa moved through Lisbon's meandering streets with exhilarating certainty. The city was suddenly novel and purposeful, free of association and full of direction, unmarred by history; another place altogether. Following a sequence of swift turns among narrow streets, Boa arrived at a vast open traffic circle. At its center, cast in bronze: a conquering hero grasping a lion.

Flying in over Lisbon, lit up with midday sun, Bourne was stunned by the epic drama of its setting. Coming here had been

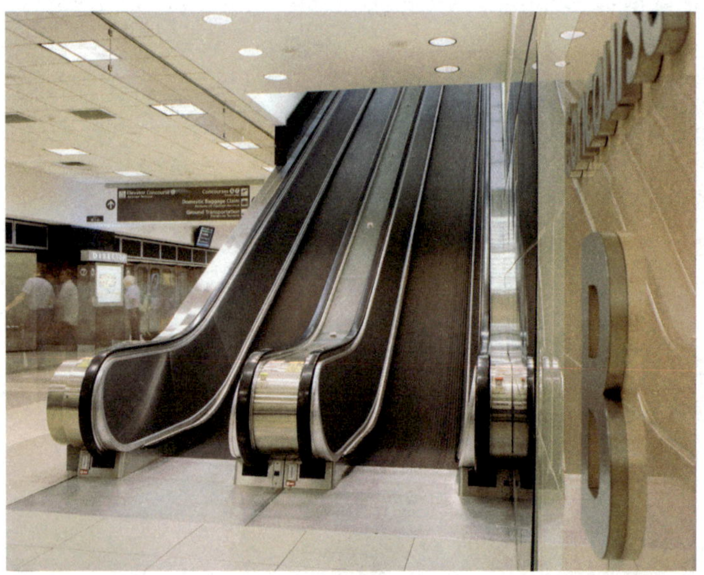

an afterthought, almost accidental. But Bourne had once read a book in which Lisbon had seemed involuted, resonant with sunken mysteries, and this heaviness appealed.

On the road from the airport, the taxi driver asked for a destination. This twin, pining for pastness, said simply: *The museum*. But peering through its enormous plate-glass doors into a succession of sleek spaces evoked the airy disorientation of home. Bourne was drawn elsewhere: south, across the lawn, towards the trees.

By the time Bourne reached the street beyond the gardens, the tug had become fantastically specific. The twin advanced like

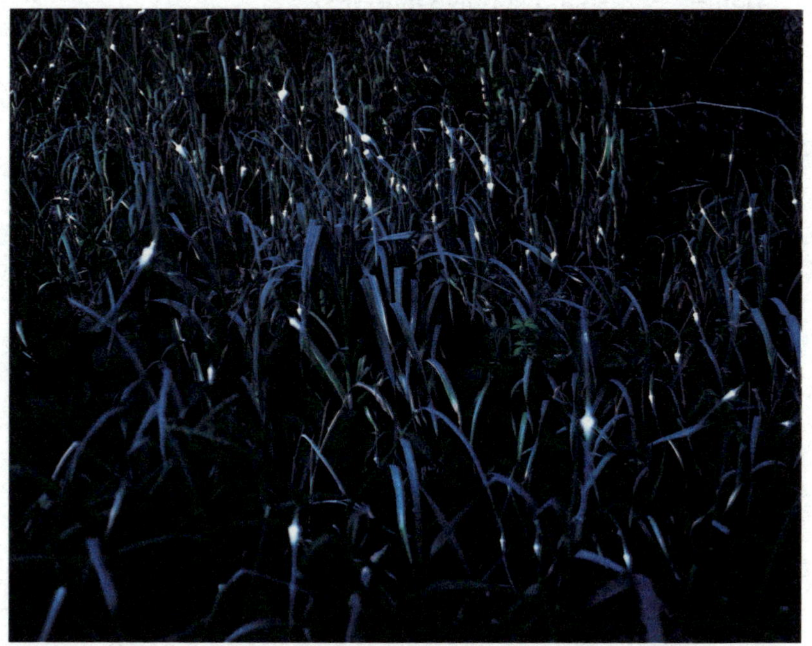

a hungry coyote at an uneven trot, buffeted by the intrusions of architecture until arriving at a wasteland of broken pavement and pale weeds. One red-dirt path cut across this emptiness, and the twin, without noting it, followed.

Minutes later, Bourne stood at the edge of a small plaza above a shrub-gridded park, with the entire city, and the sun sinking towards the sea, laid out below. Bruised and dusty, the twin rushed across the pavement, coming to a full stop before a ruinous configuration of cracked cement pilings, orphaned stone columns and a crumbling pedestal, rising from a shallow pool of water. The distant bells of the church of Saint Sebastian tolled four times. Sharp afternoon light cut into the formless construct, fractured into a thousand beams and shot forward from the silhouetted wreckage. Bourne froze in its blinding white array.

Intent on the formal landscape ahead, Boa cut northeast across the rotating traffic, taking no notice of the cars, or the monument to man and lion. The park's core was a stern grid of grass and hedge, discouraging entry. But Boa ignored the clear logic of the place, lurching over the shrubs, staggering along the increasingly steep lawns and finally clambering up a nearly vertical slope to the balustrade at the park's apex.

Boa emerged onto the sidewalk like a diver from the ocean: headfirst, breathless, exhilarated. A bell pealed four times to mark the arrival. There, on that narrow plaza, stood an arrangement of ruin: raw rock, broken pillars, splintered slabs of cement, all bathed in the erratic gush and spill of water. The sun, surging in from the coast behind, broke over Boa's back and the catastrophic monument, catching itself up in a thousand small, waterborne refractions and exploding in the eyes.

A shattered fountain, an epic pile, a splendid weightless rubble, the ruptured sundial of 4 p.m. Each twin arrested in exquisite erasure, blind antipodes, released equally from the metallic taint of nothing and the rankness of too much. Enlightened, in a moment and its light, with two astonishing impressions.

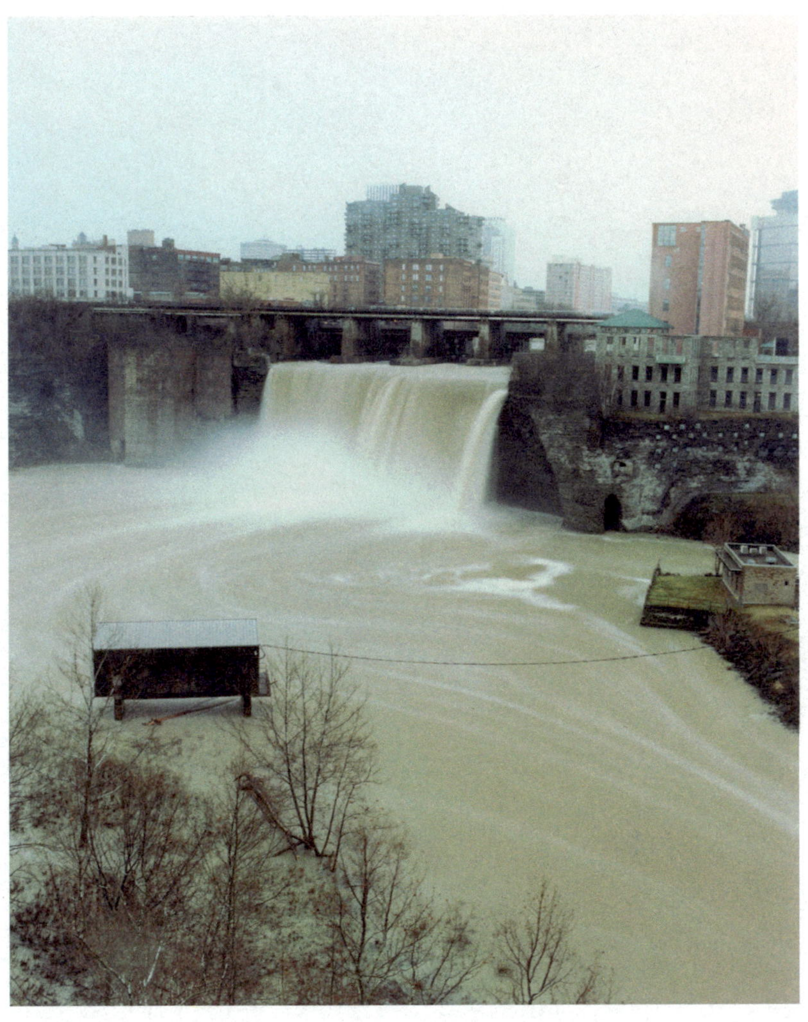

"A Tug in Lisbon" was originally published as an insert to *East of the Sun, West of the Moon* by Greg Halpern and Ahndraya Parlato, (Paris: Études Books, 2014).

V.

This Slideshow Has No Pictures

(A Visual Documentary of Psychoanalysis)

<u>**Prologue**</u>

A PICTURE: blue couch against birch-paneled wall. Centered above it, a painting. The frame: gold but not gilt. The style: casually post-impressionist, loosely daubed. The sofa is modern, in a gentle late-seventies way: knurled cotton fabric and angled bolster cushions, removable when the patient prefers to lie down. The painting suggests a turtle, bold brushstrokes rendering a shell raked in golden light, from which the green head emerges in profile, marked by a single vermillion eye. It might be titled: sunset with carapace.

ooo

I am a photographer. But over the past several years I have been interviewing psychotherapists – from psychoanalysts in private practice to psychiatrists working with mentally ill, violent offenders.

The practice of psychoanalytic psychotherapy has always embraced the seduction and power of the image, usually as source material for linguistic interpretation. Images become useful for the therapeutic process through translation into language.

For reasons both too obvious and still obscure, I want to know, as a dumb photographer, if the creation of visual images can be understood as its own form of analytical response. Do therapists, in other words, make pictures like photographers do?

In these interviews I seek to document the invisible visual content of therapists' work with patients, beginning with the seemingly straightforward question: what do you see in your imagination when patients talk to you? From here, I have accumulated both a catalog of visual descriptions – verbal pictures – from the therapists' imaginaries, and a series of often revealing narratives about the interpretive efficacies, dangers and challenges of

59

these images within therapeutic work. The material of this visual documentary is, for me, a collection of photographs that aren't pictured: a portrait of a process that is both image-driven and innately immaterial. What follows are some episodes from this still-unfolding fieldwork.

ooo

"Just this wall, this completely bricked-up wall, that was right behind her, that had no options, that you couldn't climb up or get over, that entirely sealed the room."

The psychiatrist had this image ready for me, because she thought I might ask her for something. She visualized it every time she met with a certain patient: a woman who had done something terrible and irrevocable, and whose anguish was irremediable. The "wall of impossibility," as the psychiatrist called it, was insurmountable: "You couldn't chip it down, you couldn't climb up it, it was just this solid huge thing."

Occasionally, in place of the wall, she visualized the room filled up with insulation foam: "There's nowhere to breathe, there's nothing happening and there's no air; there's no movement."

The patients she worked with had all committed violent crimes, and they arrived to her with not only a history, but one or more "index offenses" around which their life stories had been reordered. Their lives seemed to open out, forward and back, from these terrible definitive moments.

I asked if she visualizes these dramatic past events. "I imagine them," she said, "as if it's a film."

Interested, I sought to clarify: so you see movement rather than fixed images?

Both, she said, reconsidering. "Probably a lot of it is fixed scenes. In fact, even when I think it's a film, it's probably just a series of fixed scenes. Because there's lots you don't know."

"And they're not necessarily straight on," she continued. "One patient in particular, when I try to imagine his index offense, it's as if it's happening over to the side. Like a really bad photograph that someone's taken with a snappy camera at a social occasion, where you can see people in it, but they're not facing the camera."

And why, I wondered, do you think you view *that* event in *this* way?

"It's almost as if I don't want to see him doing what he did, as if I'm saying: well, it's not that clear what happened. Part of me wants to understand that he's a very damaged boy. It's partly because of my sympathy that I can't see the whole thing."

Persistently and vividly, this therapist spoke about interiors. If she was interested in a particular case, she explained, she would have not only the patient's figure in her mind, but the layout of a building, or of a room. I asked if these spaces were drawn from research: police narratives, evidence photographs, patient descriptions?

Mostly, she said, realizing the answer as it came from her mouth, I invent them.

In one case, her visualization often began with a view of a doorway to the patient's kitchen, with shoes lying around, and part of the breakfast room visible beyond. "I've seen a picture of the outside," she noted. "I've had to imagine the inside." And here she caught herself: "It's interesting that I said 'had to imagine the inside'; I hadn't *had to* imagine the inside at all."

She continued, amazed: "Actually, now that I think about it, I'm always trying to come up with a floor plan. And I've always got exactly the building in my mind; maybe even the trees outside the windows; even the type of kitchen furnishings." She burst out in a sharp laugh of recognition as more detail spilled out: "The bathroom is dated and really the sort of colors that need to be ripped out and replaced – like avocado or light blue, something a bit 1970s or 1980s. In my mind, there's a carpet as well, which is old fashioned, isn't it, to have carpet? No one has carpet anymore."

She described another patient's kitchen, which she also knew nothing about: "Country kitchen effect: pine-fitted, where everything really matches but is really horrible, and you get this very shiny orange pine thing going on when you walk in."

Repeatedly, I ask: why that particular image? Repeatedly she answers: "I don't know!"

I ask if these images develop as the therapy progresses. She replies, architecturally: "I guess you have a basic structure, and the more that you learn, the more you're filling it in, so it becomes more solid. It starts sketchy, and then the detail is added on, like a scaffolding that you're amending or modifying. There are always blurred bits as to what has happened, but my mind seems to want to fill it in; to create texture and to create a scene, so that I can understand what happened."

ooo

In London, I met with a psychiatrist, not as a patient, but to ask him some questions: an interview. Nonetheless, he seated me in the patient's chair and assumed his position in the consulting chair, with the brooding blank length of the psychoanalytic couch laid out between us, gaping and suggestive in unutterable ways.

I asked him to describe what he saw when a patient told him a story – a dream, a memory, a recent event. I clarified: What does the image look like in your imagination, either in a specific case, or in general?

He answered: "I try to avoid seeing images. If I make an image, I am not thinking with my patient."

I asked him if patients ever brought in photographs to show him. Yes, he said, but he did not like it. The photograph, he suggested, is usually a form of resistance – resistance to the analyst seeing or understanding whatever he wants. The image, in other words, obfuscates.

I asked him about the space between what the patient wants to describe, and what he, the therapist, is able to discern.

Sometimes, he said, there is an image present that he cannot see. But his inability to visualize it does not mean it isn't there.

ooo

A picture: In an otherwise typical Victorian house, the windows of the ground floor are shuttered on the inside. This peculiar architectural inversion is designed as much to prevent looking in as it is to forestall peering out. The slats on these shutters are drawn down and painted shut with an interior eggshell white. But there is one window, cut into an irregular shape by the descending staircase, where a sun-faded Marimekko curtain has to do instead. From this slightly elevated vantage, a child could part the fabric and stare down upon the receding heads of his father's patients as they step up the basement stairs and disappear around the bend of a narrow, fenced path at the back of the house. While it is equally possible to catch those strangers' arriving faces, even a child of seven knows that to see them fully, frontally, is one transgression too far.

Witnessing those faceless heads – rising like solitary balloons and just as quickly receding – it is impossible not to wonder what those roundish receptacles hold. The child could, perhaps, imagine the pictures they carried of that office's semi-alien terrain:

always several degrees cooler and several decades starker than the sentimental jumble above. But the images that unfold from those heads into the father's consciousness, and the pictures that he sends back to the strangers' waiting minds — that parade of shared and shifting tableaux passing just below the floorboards — is undeniable and unimaginable.

ooo

He began with the flashes: "I don't like to go downstairs and open the door and not know which patient is there. I like to know, because often I have an image right before the hour starts."

What do these images look like, I asked.

"Sometimes," he explained, "it's a scene, or it has a darkness to it. Images like: on a river at dusk." At this moment, as he talked, a peal of church bells began in the distance. "Sometimes it explains to me what's been going on; sometimes it's predictive; not in a mystical way, but because I'm getting something."

Often, he continued, it reflects a mood, "because a mood can be translated into an image. It could be my mood, but most of the time it's the mood that the patient has been in, or is working their way out of or into." Here he talked about light, color, space — the aesthetic vocabulary of visual tone.

This flash, what he calls "having a visual image before an hour" is both "remembering and anticipatory: remembering what was probably most important, turned into an image, and anticipating what I should focus on, what I need to remember to keep the framework of the whole process going where it's going."

When asked about his method of responding to patients' narratives in the hour, his answer was emphatic: "The minute I'm hearing anything, I'm seeing things at the same time. I can't help it; it just happens."

"To me," he elaborated, "images are inherently richer than a couple of words. So I certainly consider them equal, if not more valuable." But sometimes, he acknowledged, "they're a counter, a defense, a way of not feeling something painful – something funny, for instance, in place of something that hurts. Sometimes the image is a way to understand, but it represents interference with understanding, too."

Throughout our conversation, the analyst's vocabulary was infused with optical and chemical processes. "Sometimes," he began, "you may just hear of it like a particular small snapshot," one that the patient brings up and just as quickly wants to dismiss. Often, he said, there is a bit of a struggle to tease it out. He called this "the push and pull to getting it developed." It was a language that echoed my old experience of the darkroom. "You may work on developing one picture for months," he explained, "or you may do it within 15 minutes. Some pictures take a long time. It's a bit like you're fiddling around with a microscope. You look on low power and high power and you hold it up to the light. You look at it from different angles and you work at it together. You make the image come into existence."

Time and the tape were running out, and an impulse pushed me to shift our focus. Why, I asked, do you think a photographer is asking you these questions?

"Photography," he responded, "is always about imagery. How people use it and struggle with it and change it and value it and devalue and are threatened by it. In photography, you make images, you don't just click, you do things with them, too, and you have to work with yourself about that. The overt aim is different, but underneath, they're cousins.

"Finding ways to produce affect-laden reactions: strong, powerful reactions, things that put people in touch with something about themselves or their lives. That's what I try to do and what you try to do."

ooo

In London, I met with a psychiatrist, not as a patient, but to ask him some questions: an interview. He bought me coffee; we talked across a table in an empty seminar room.

I asked him about his work with violent offenders, and the relationship between evidence photographs and the patients' descriptions of events.

The photographs, he noted, are absolutely static. In the mental images suggested by patients one can feel their movement – they are fluid, not fixed. The photographs are depleted. They never conform to the image that one has because the image is very different: It isn't a photograph.

ooo

It happened several times in my childhood: my father and I were walking in our neighborhood when he spotted a patient approaching from afar. Each time, he told me, with some urgency, to cross the street and walk on alone. Afterwards, he would catch me up at a trot, his pressed wool slacks flapping around his ankles, and we would continue on. Once I asked if the patient did not know that he had children. My father explained: it was much more important to know how the patients *imagined* his family. If they could see me, they wouldn't have to invent me. To become a good image, I had to remain invisible.

ooo

In London, I met with a psychiatrist, not as a patient, but to ask her some questions: an interview. Nonetheless, she seated me in the patient's chair and assumed her position in the consulting chair, halfway across the office. I observed her desk, her books, the abstract paintings and landscape posters on the wall.

I asked her to describe her patients' accounts of memories, events and dreams. Were they cinematic or photographic; were they narratively or visually seductive?

Rarely, she said.

What struck her most about her patients' imaginative lives was their unillustrated blankness. Often, the signal fact was the lack of images. She described one patient in particular who almost never generated images that she could visualize or discuss. The patient, she said, was almost like a ghost.

Often, she said, the patients' images were marked by absence rather than richness, bleakness rather than seduction. But absence, she cautioned, is itself a kind of image.

ooo

Unlike the first Lacanian analyst I met with, the second one was not also, secretly, a photographer. But like her predecessor, she started by insisting that the image had no useful place in her clinical practice. This refusal began, subtly, in the email exchange preceding our meeting. She wrote: "I'm not sure if I'll be able to help you, but we can talk." And from the moment I followed her through a narrow, elegant doorway into a tastefully appointed office, this point of view became more clear: "Let me say straight away that it is very mysterious to me, your question, because as a Lacanian psychoanalyst, we work on words, so I don't have images in my mind forming when I speak to patients. I listen to the words. And I try to isolate series of logical terms that are related to each other. And I try to divorce them from the meaning that they think their story has to tell, and to find out what the meaning is that they don't know that their story has."

In her elaboration of this process, the image was, initially, the problem. An image, she insisted, "is a totality. It's constructed as a whole, and you can't interact with it in any way. It's there." Language offers a potential for freedom absent in the image, because a sentence, and even a word, can be taken apart and rearranged.

And this, I asked her, is not possible with an image? Images, she insisted, are scenarios; scenarios are screens; screens obfuscate.

And yet, somehow, despite this, and in fact, over and over again, the visual, and visualizations even, kept creeping in. Speaking of the dynamism that childhood memories gain once the psychoanalytic process has taken hold, she enthused: "It's amazing, because when they're caught up with the experience of the analysis, those scenes take on different meanings and different interpretations, and you see different things at different times, from different perspectives and different angles."

Speaking of a patient: "At the moment I do visualize him putting on the character like an outfit. Because that's what he does; that's what I imagine him doing."

Despite this effusion, she persisted: "Every image is a screen. A screen that conceals the truth of your enjoyment; the beautiful image is concealing a fairly banal and non-glamorous mode of enjoyment. The analyst" – and here it was impossible not to think of the *Wizard of Oz* – "has to take you behind the screen, behind the image."

"But," I too persisted, "this other reality, the hidden and less glamorous one, why is that not also an image?" She paused for a few seconds – what seemed, for her, an eternity without language:

"Because it doesn't have a scenario. It's just an enjoyment, of seeing the other reduced to nothingness."

Of what she calls "the phantasmic representation of yourself" she explains, "as an analyst, our job is to break that down and to show what's behind that image."

I wonder, but do not ask: what is a show without an image?

The analyst gave another example of "what an image can conceal," but this one seemed to slip away from her. An artist-patient had talked about a traumatic event for a long time. But it was only once she discovered that she had, without intending to, represented the trauma in an artwork, that she could move on. "What is an image?" the analyst asked herself again. "It's not distinct from words. It exceeds words. It's more than words." Now, in the image, the trauma "was contained and framed, it was in its place" and the patient was free from it. "Some things can't be moved in language," she observed, "they are too heavy. I suppose an image, in that sense, is a way to do that."

Refocusing her eyes on me, she remarked, archly, in the way of people who feel they've been tricked, "Well, it appears you have psychoanalyzed me!"

ooo

We met at 17, our first week of college: two teens imagining themselves artists. Decades later, we sit down in her Manhattan office to talk. Behind her head, centered above the psychoanalytic couch, hangs one of my photographs, carefully selected by her many years ago for this position. A dense color landscape image clogged with undergrowth, it deliberately frustrates the urge to focus, foreclosing the illusion of perspective. A picture of impenetrable space.

The interview begins, at first haltingly, and then more freely. Once, she tells me, she caught herself mis-imagining a patient's dream about her, and what she had seen, not heard, was important. As she vividly describes the two different pictures – the patient's and her own – I suddenly notice that the photograph above the couch has started to peel away from its support, the paper lifting free of the permanent adhesive to curl up ever so slightly at one corner. My image, in her office, had begun to come unstuck.

ooo

Recently, towards the end of an hour, I tell my therapist that I've been wondering about interviewing him.

He asks what I've been *wondering* and what I would want to ask?

Here I am careful to answer professionally, generally, as I always do as an interviewer: I would ask about the images he sees, in his mind, when talking to patients.

But he responds more pointedly: "Do you want to know about *my* images when talking with *you*?"

I freeze, in unanticipated panic, as if I had thought this question could pass undetected. I can feel a threshold being broken: the picture plane that I've imagined sliding out of my control. Finally, automatically, I answer: "I don't believe I want to know."

Suddenly, there is a secret animating the room. He looks right at me, then turns momentarily away. He says nothing. He has seen something, but he cannot find the words. The time is up. As I stand to leave, I cannot help but notice small tears forming at the edges of his eyes.

ooo

I was 13. We were in the middle of a typically fractious family dinner, when, for reasons now forgotten, I referred to the painting of the turtle above the couch in my father's office. A moment of silent confusion was followed by an eruption of laughter. That painting – a turtle? I attempted to explain what was to me so obvious: the red–brown shell, its green head and livid eye. But to the other five people at the table, initially too full of humiliating merriment to respond clearly, my delusion was extraordinary and evident. It was merely a mountainous landscape; the animal's "head" – a patch of green pasture. This truth was undeniable. I could no more reject their mountain than my turtle. The image was a shell and a vista.

ooo

In London, one psychoanalyst gave me a picture I don't want to shake. He said, the patient and I enter together into the scene, as if going with a child by the hand.

"This Slideshow Has No Pictures" was originally published in *Embodied Encounters: New Approaches to Psychoanalysis and Film*, edited by Agnieszka Piotrowska, (New York and Oxford: Routledge, 2014).

VI.

No Such Place

A fiction for the photographs of Ron Jude

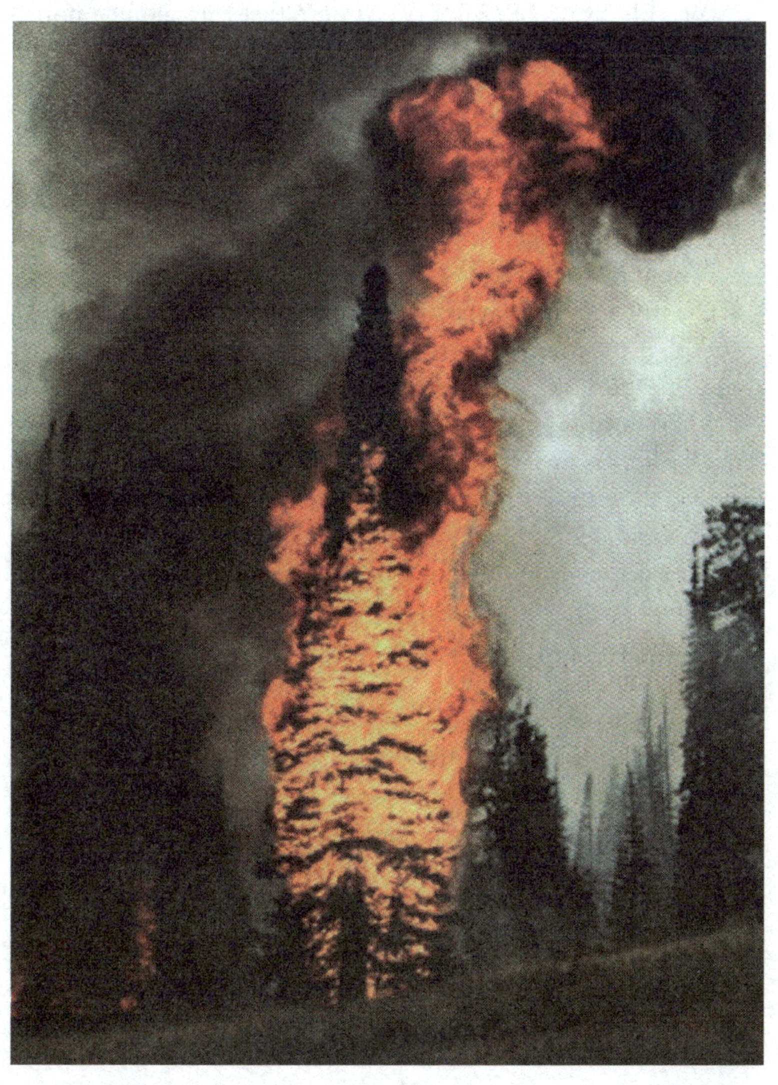

I.

WHEN YOU LIVE IN A VALLEY that runs along a north-south axis, the beginning and end of things take on a certain symmetry. At dawn, the sun rises behind the eastern range, casting a sharp silhouette of burning light on to the western ridge. At dusk, the eastern peaks are suddenly lit with the stark outline of the western summits. As the Oracle says, you know that you live in a valley only when standing in shadow.

The two ranges trade images of each other most visibly on brilliant winter days, when the snow and the sharpness of light conspire for ideal projection. It was in the very middle of just such a December day that Sue appeared at my door. She was the town's code enforcement officer, and had come to inspect my house, on the western edge of town, before allowing some walls to be knocked down. Sue was gentle in demeanor, solid in stature and her respect for the rule of law was leavened only by her respect for neighborly consideration. She was an enforcer of common sense and had the kind of thick oversized plastic glasses that only a rural code enforcement officer could wear without either a whiff of irony or a twinge of tragedy. Sue carried herself with dignity.

In her early years on the job, as Sue walked through houses, room by room and floor by floor, the owners would follow and talk. The styles of monologue varied, from urgent chatter to lanky tales, unfolding in lengths like a collapsible yardstick. They talked to ward off the taint of criminality that accompanies even the most innocent inspection. They talked because they had something to hide, even if they had no idea what that thing might be. In the process, of course, they gave all kinds of information away. Most of it was junk, and this suited Sue just fine — an irrelevant talk-radio backdrop to her focused inspection. Occasionally, though, more valuable transmissions came through: scraps of fact and bits of story from the increasingly interconnected lore of the town.

Sometimes, at the end of her inspections, people showed her photographs. Sue was so nearsighted that she didn't remove her weighty frames to look at even the tiniest image. She simply held it at arm's length and adjusted the focal length through contractions of her elbow – the way stereographic views were adjusted forward and back along a rail to achieve the proper illusion of depth in the viewing device.

The more Sue learned, the more she talked; the more she talked, the less she wrote things down. By the time Sue arrived at my house, she had crossed over fully from data collector to storyteller. The mountains were visible from every house in the valley, and Sue's particular fascination – one secretly shared by the whole town – was the story of the abandoned upland settlements. As I followed her around my house, fearing the imminent eruption of some unknown scandal of substandard construction, I gladly fell under the spell of her narrative.

Comfort Peak, above the east side of the town, and Forge Mountain, atop the western flank of the valley, were settled around the mines. These were company towns – one on each ridge – carved out against clear-cut slopes and strung together by steep mountain roads and complex intermarriages. After the First World War, the markets slumped and production slowed. Eventually the company went bankrupt, ceding the land to the federal government and leaving the mining families behind in their houses. Years later, the government bought the remaining residents out of their homes, razed the town, and resettled everyone in the surrounding lowlands. The barren slopes were reforested and converted into wilderness land. All that remained of the settlements were isolated foundations, roads converted into hiking trails, and a few abandoned cemeteries. Seventy years later, the hills are uninhabited.

Sue had begun to share her research with a guy named Wade, who lived on the far side of the valley from me, all the way east, where the sun sets an hour later. Sue was adept at organizing and cataloguing facts, but Wade was the culler and keeper of photographs. He was descended from mining families, and pictures are the kinds of things people prefer to share with kin. So when I asked Sue if there were photographs from the old settlements, she said: You would have to speak to Wade.

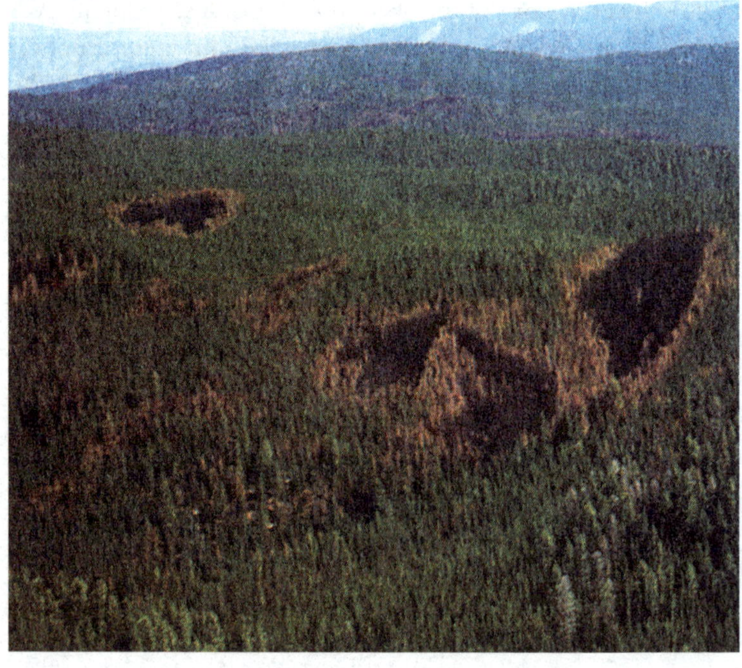

II.

Wade's house is the only habitable structure at the spot where Ridge Road drops down to meet School Road in a sudden tee. It's a low-slung split-level home set among two crumpled wooden chicken houses, a massive dark barn and a couple of small, indefinite outbuildings. Wade emerged out of some tall brush at the edge of a manicured lawn as I pulled into the driveway. He carried a big empty bucket that looked delicate in his enormous hands. Inside, after a twilight tour of his fossil and brick collections, Wade seemed a bit too large for the low-ceilinged kitchen he led me through en route to the living room.

He called it, with a wink, the "Board Room," and it was indeed dominated by an enormous dry-erase board, about 14-feet long and 4-feet tall. Set atop three folding tables, and propped against the mantelpiece, the board nearly touched the ceiling. On it, Wade and Sue had mapped out the entire genealogy of the mountain towns. Every known member of each recorded family was listed in neat columns, decorated with a serpentine of bright orange lines indicating marriages. This genealogy, and the folkloric saga that unfurled around it, painted Forge Mountain and Comfort Peak as one continuous world. The two upland settlements seemed inseparable, linked by families and traditions, as if the two mines met in a deep subterranean passageway. The mountain people were like flying squirrels gliding over the inconsequential valley floor; dust-bowl brigands, signaling back and forth across the shadowy chasm.

On the largest Formica tabletop I have ever seen, among the mounds and spreads of notes and letters and other informational flotsam, were two enormous binders, tabbed with the surnames of all the families. Some names were mundane: Smith and Powers and O'Brien. Many offered a frankly materialist directness: House and Bucket, Longhouse and Bastion; Messenger, Bacon and Fish.

Finally, there was a flurry of wondrously conditional families, blurred into uncertainty from their very inceptions: Parshall, Slighter, Mabee and Mabie. These were the faces I wanted to see.

Wade waved me to a seat, forged a clearing on the table, and set the first binder in front of me. I opened it, and there they were: newlyweds, sixth-grade classes, family gatherings, schoolyard high jinks, snowy landscapes and summery idylls. Clapboard houses with back porches, smart little schoolhouses with pastured horses. A catalogue of facades, back yards and front parlors. There was no dignified squalor or hard-bitten deprivation. No mud and pride and resignation. I saw no malnourished children of careworn mothers, whose windswept faces stared into uncertain futures. I looked through the entirety of both albums, but not a soul even looked tired. As the Oracle says, the peaks had been purged only of happiness.

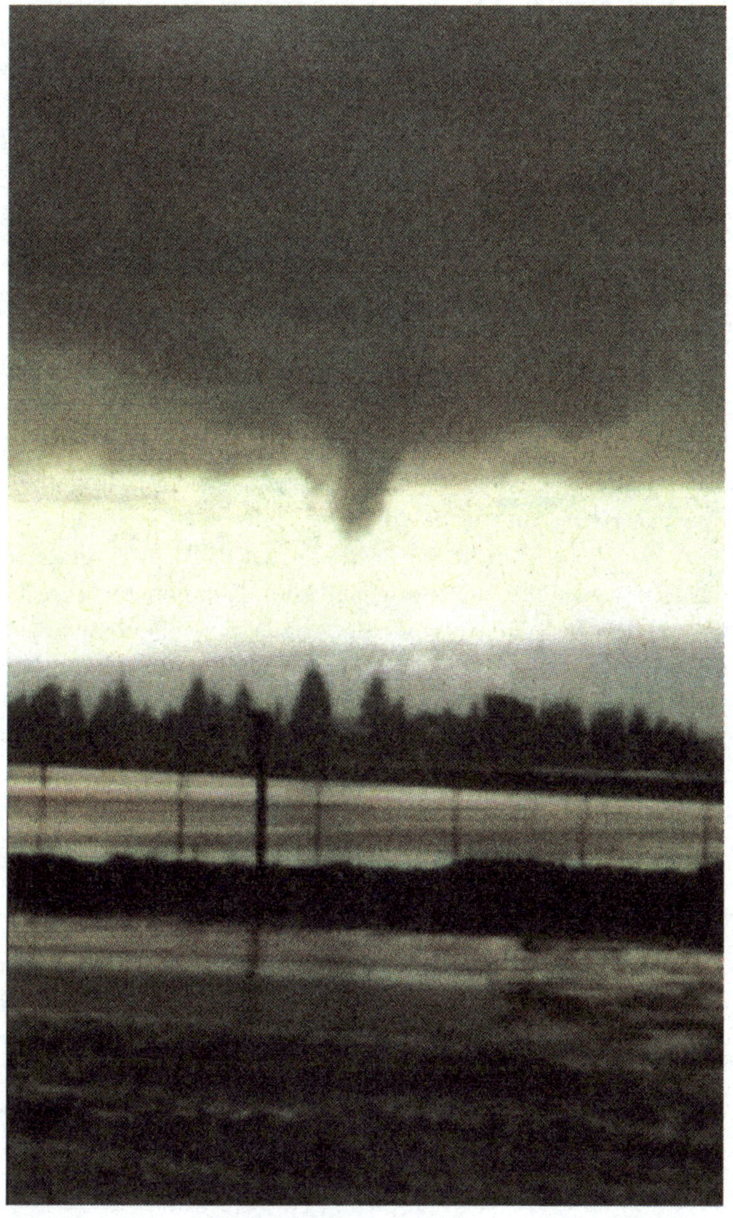

III.

A few mornings after her first visit, Sue stopped by my house again. There were a few things she had overlooked or forgotten; stuff she had not written down. I said: You were telling me too many stories. She sheepishly agreed. And in an uncharacteristic moment of neighborly self-regard, I said: Next time you go out on inspections, I will come along and take pictures for you, for reference. She laughed awkwardly and declined. I persisted, asking what she was doing the rest of the day. She answered — reluctantly, and because she wasn't much for lying — that she had a few inspections. This was my chance. I said: I'm free right now. I'll come with you, as your assistant. She didn't know what to do. She accepted the offer. I grabbed my camera and followed in my own car, giving Sue her due distance.

As we went from house to house that day, I photographed whatever Sue looked at — a camera flash of light punctuating each observation. Usually she would nod towards the offending object or area, or, most helpfully, and sometimes with my prodding, point to it with her gently crimped index finger. Sue obviously didn't enjoy the awkwardness of my presence and the invasiveness of the camera. It undermined her private rapport with the home-owners, and she was more reticent than usual. Still, Sue told a few stories, and I listened while I shot, drunk on the conjoined pleasures of inclusion and distance. I knew, already, that this would never happen again.

Sue described a spot, far from the remaining road on Comfort Peak, where the mine manager's house once stood. The federal government had razed the structure, but left the wisteria vines, which had been trained up through the porch columns, to run wild. Every spring, in the deep obscurity of the forest, this giant undomesticated vine erupts in a baroque mass of violet flowers twining among the treetops. As the Oracle says, there is always wisteria in the woods.

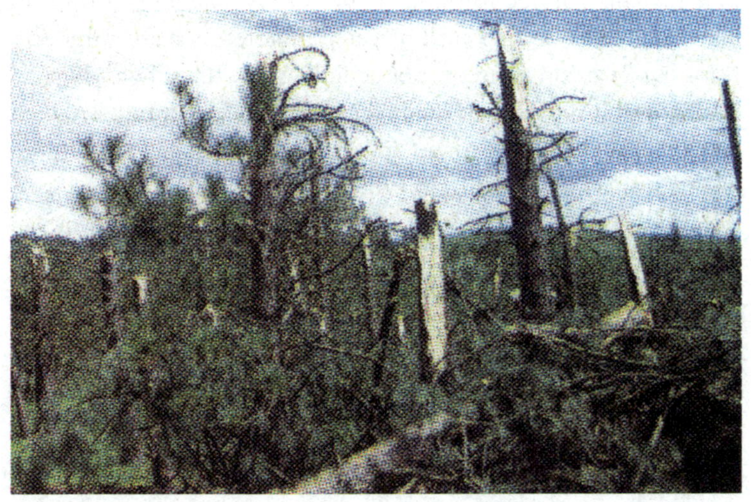

IV.

Sue sits at her computer, between the wood stove and the upright piano, in that great dark room at the back of her house. Her dial-up connection churns heroically, like an old mill ox, painstakingly unveiling each picture, a quarter inch at a time. She leans in towards the screen, her mouth agape, the slowly alternating ratio of luminance to shadow playing across her bespectacled face. The scene seems to last forever – a Caravaggesque rendering of some minor myth, in which the horror and splendor of her astonished visage, lit by a primitive forge, supersedes the particulars of the obscure narrative.

Late at night, there is an email reply from Sue. The subject line is blank. I open it. The message is three words long, in all caps, in royal blue.

OH I NO.

I scroll down but there is nothing else. I read it over and over again, speaking it under my breath. The syntax of these three words seems impenetrable. Oh I no. The utterance suggests resignation. Then it sounds like sarcasm and rebuke. Finally, the phrase settles into a dark incantation: an assertion, a curse and an accusation. It is a chant in a mysterious ritual. Urgent breathy sounds to summon unknown forces.

OH I NO. OH I NO. OH I NO.

Outside, in the sharp December night, cold air catches in the lungs like a sudden affliction. The town, held in the valley, is extinguished completely. But the snow-dusted peaks throb into presence, shadowy bitmaps of low-res grandeur, gathering faint light from unknown sources. Orion is laid out in unnatural clarity above the eastern ridge. Just below, not in the sky but on the mountaintop, is an unexpected glimmer. This light quavers and moves, as if held aloft by a desperate fugitive, or a mad hunter giving chase. The unsteady beam warbles briefly along the ridge, moving south through haphazard wilderness, and disappears.

In the restored stillness, Comfort Peak and Forge Mountain hum solemnly, the tones meeting in a minor discord that descends to resonate along the valley floor. As the Oracle says, these lowlands hold no harmony.

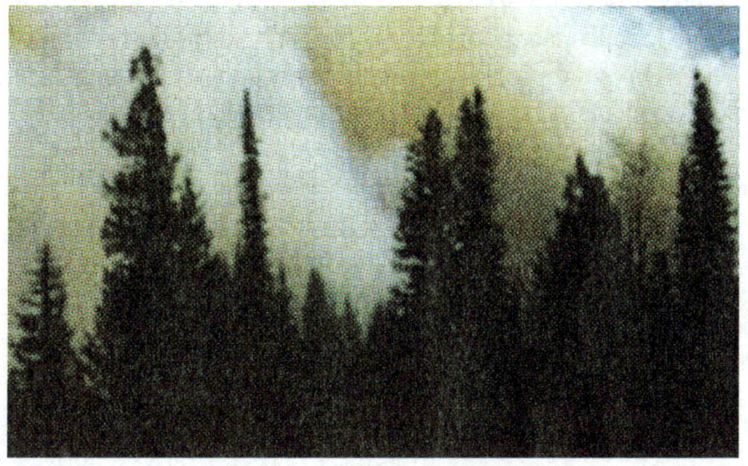

V.

1. Raw harrowing confusion. What seems to be the overbright arch of an arm ending in a partially severed hand. Behind that, the back of a cave, or perhaps a basement: alternating dark masses that resolve only into obscurity.

2. The upper half of a framed poster. Above it, a gray wall joins an equally gray ceiling. The left side of a face appears in the right foreground, radically unfocussed, light blocking the eye and revealing only the jagged line between brown bangs and white forehead.

3. From above, the back of a figure, dropping into a murky stair-well, as if reeling downward after a sharp blow. In the fore-ground, on the wall, black scuff marks indicate a struggle.

4. A suddenly turned back, caught in the glare of illumination. Behind and to the left, in profile, one arm outstretched in zombie somnolence, the figure moves across spectral darkness.

5. The corner of a wooden dresser. Motes of dust caught up in the sudden light. Behind that, a soiled-looking bed and a crouch-ing figure, signaling urgently toward the floor.

6. A jaw and a mouth – set neutrally, with a gentle downward frown. Above the nose, the twin orbs of giant glasses concentrate all the obliterating light of a horrible flash. Around them, nothing.

7. A curved drainpipe drops into the center of the frame, so lit as to suggest electrification. It is met and gripped, erotically, between thumb and forefinger.

8. A blurred forearm ending in a small hand, curled almost into a fist. Behind it, sharp but in shadow, a jagged dark hole in a white wall, revealing sinews of wood and metal.

"No Such Place" was originally published in *Lick Creek Line* by Ron Jude, (London: Mack Books, 2012).

VII.
Another Minor Avant-Garde

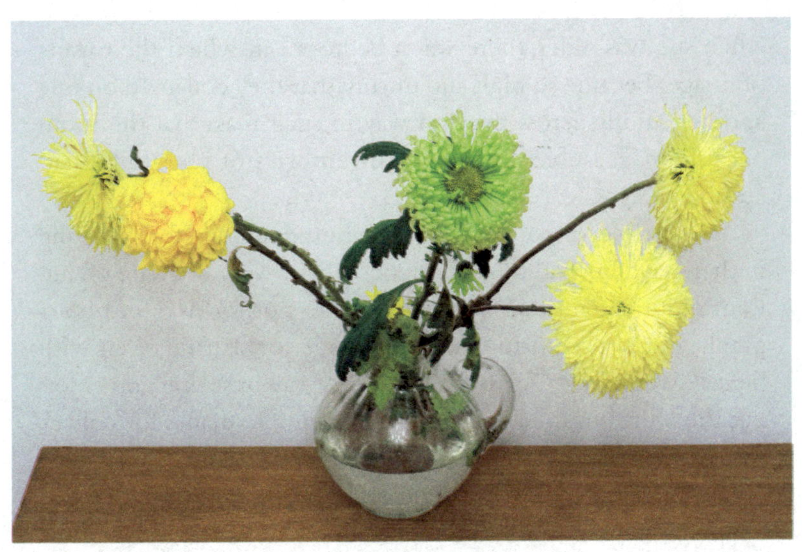

GRANDMOTHER ANNE (for that is how she signed our birthday cards) had trouble remembering our names, and she could never really recall our ages. Grandmother was not a role she relished, or perhaps, even, accepted. I imagine that, if I met her now, I might admire her independence, but that feminist perspective was not available to me as a child. She liked to travel, and look at art, and make *ikebana* floral arrangements. She did not enjoy her family. But she loved to photograph. She had beautiful camera equipment that we were not allowed to touch, and she would occasionally, unexpectedly, take pictures at family gatherings. But except for one or two photographs from a rare family reunion (images made memorable by the command by which she organized the portrait: "Everyone, up against the wall!"), I can't remember viewing a single photograph she took. I *saw* her photographs, though. Mountains of them, in slide boxes and carousels, reaching in deranged, toppling towers towards the ceiling. First in her house, and then again in the apartment she moved into when she was older, there was a bedroom in which the towers of images became so high and unruly that they collapsed on one another, falling across the doorway in such mass that the room became inaccessible. Enormous inventories of physically inaccessible images.

It's possible, of course, that her photographs, before arriving in that mayhem, had other audiences that I was not aware of, but I am quite certain that her images were not for us. Her photographs did not seem to have been made for sharing, even with herself. Were they a form of capture? A way of seeing and enjoying the world in the act of making? A simple mania for collecting, matching her compulsion to store decades of daily *Boston Globes* in her garage – a hoarding of the world in images? Even as children we used to joke about her unseen pictures; if Grandma photographed something, we were certain never to see it! The photograph was almost a guarantee of disappearance, as if her obsession was murderous. As if she wanted to render the visible world, so as to destroy and forget it.

Grandmother Anne once gave my then four-year-old cousin a large wrapped box for her birthday. As we all looked on, the excited child ripped open the present to find a smaller box inside. Within that box, another, still smaller, and then another and another. Inside the last box, there was nothing. That was her gift.

VIII.
Mountain Shadow Place

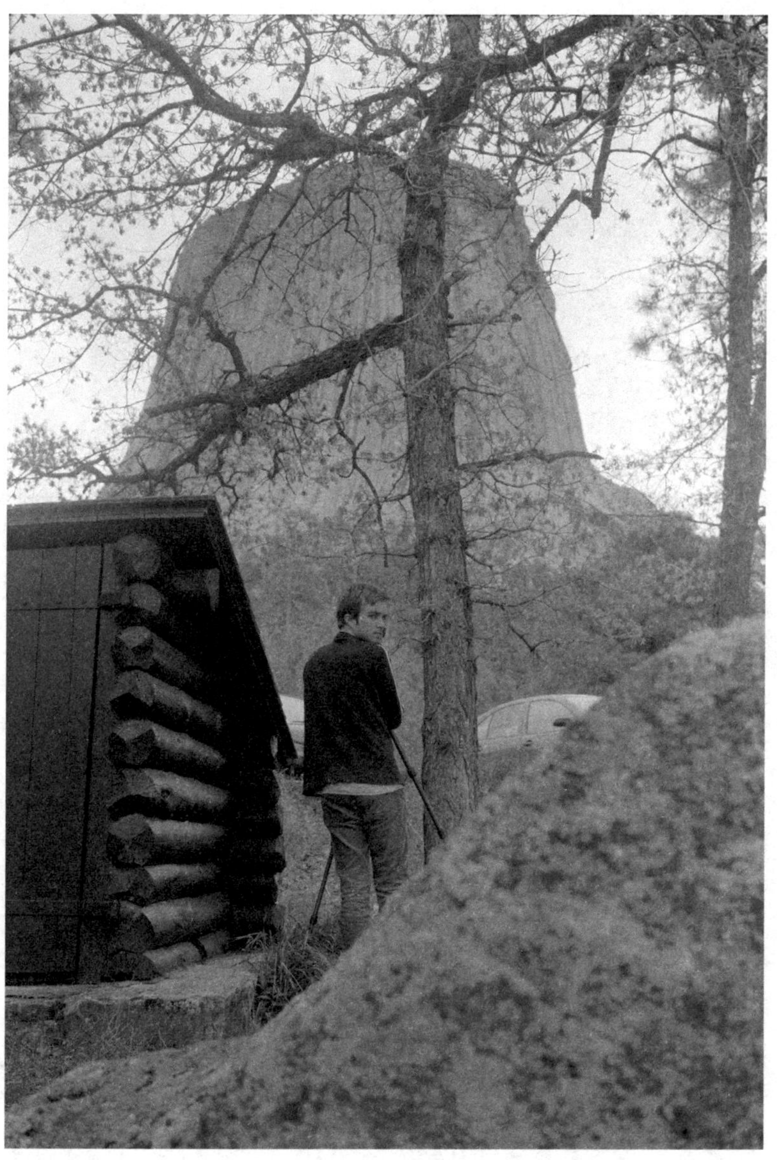

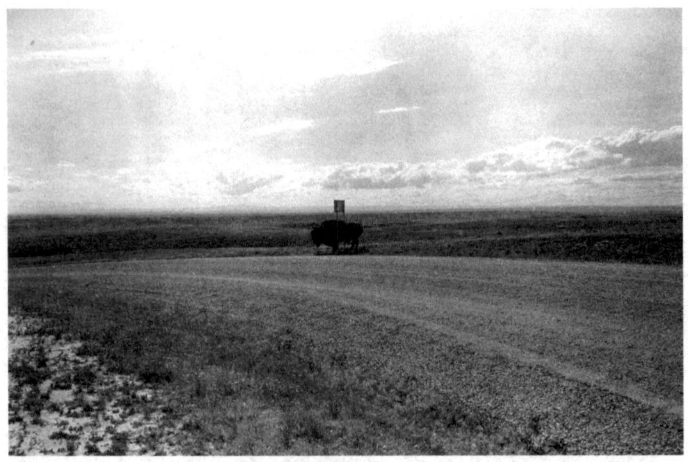

TWO MEN AND THEIR DOG. We entered the Badlands National Park at dusk, setting up camp against the fading sun. One small cluster of tents stood across the campground, their inhabitants unintelligible in the semi-monochrome of settling darkness. Distant buffalo grazed or stood or slept, standing, along the high ridge above the site. We ate and turned in early.

Night was broken by the clatter and flash of an electrical storm, followed by a steady rain. At dawn, I unzipped a corner of the tent's window to assess the scene. Peeling back the moist nylon, a transformed landscape appeared: rivulets of mud transecting the prairie, and a looming congregation of sodden buffalo surrounding our tent. The dog saw this, too, and nearly lost his mind, crying and yelping with inchoate excitement, throwing his whole black body wildly against the flimsy green membrane of the tent. Outside, on a leash, confounded by the dual urges to cower and give chase, the hound walked cautiously across the wet grasses, as if entranced. The buffalo followed at a vigilant distance, circling us as we circled the tent, in a funny concentric dance of various wet beasts.

We pulled up stakes and retreated in the downpour to a Rapid City Holiday Inn.

After three days of dank seclusion, the sun appeared, brilliantly, on the fourth. We jumped in the car and drove towards Devils Tower – that iconic flat-topped monolith from *Close Encounters* – just across the Wyoming border.

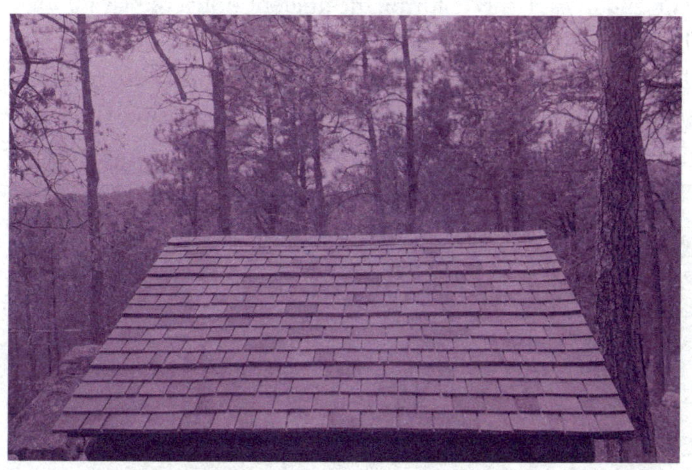

An hour later, the near hills dropped away from the high-way and the Tower appeared, fantastical in the distance. We exited north, in its direction. But the giant and strangely geometric object seemed to stay in place, flat and remote, as we approached. Twenty minutes passed, and it was unmoved, shimmering insolently in its vast rectitude. The Tower's strange vertical insistence, refusing to diminish towards a summit, and its defiant incongruity against the low landscape, meant that any estimation of scale was impossi-ble, or ridiculously speculative. Finally, we reached the base of the park road, which turned gently uphill into a forest. There, where the sign read "Devils Tower," Devils Tower disappeared.

We emerged from the sinuous forest road onto a parking lot. To the right, a visitor's center and some park offices. To the left, that enormous rock – spectacularly close, but no less difficult to apprehend – like a movie star suddenly entering an elevator. We parked and proceeded into this scene – of fantasy collaged against realism – on foot. An informational plaque at the trailhead sought to explain the mysterious column: the ancient impacted lava flow of a subterranean volcano, around which weaker stone had slowly eroded. We circled the tower's base. Periodically, miniature mountaineers appeared on the rock face, dangling from invisible threads at still unmeasurable heights: part way up, towards the top, somewhere in the middle.

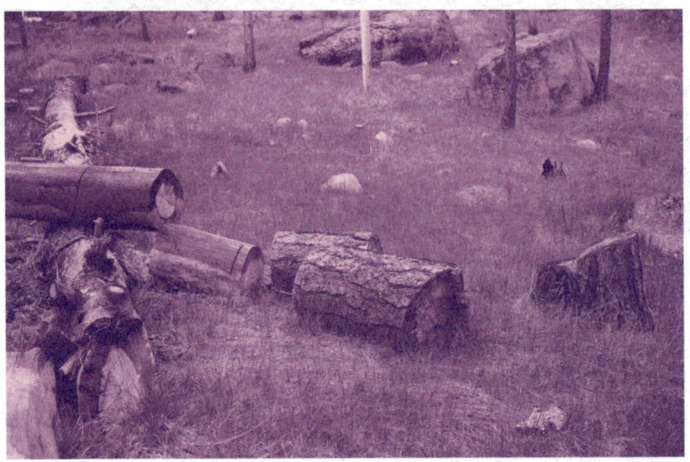

It felt as if the time-space continuum had abandoned these climbers in contempt at their absurd acts of will: indignant physics hanging them out to dry, without chronology or depth. I imagined they would be there, tiny and suspended, forever. And if they ever did reach the top, what manner of transcendence would they achieve on the tiny flat prairie that the retreating world had left behind? How would it feel to command such a view but to be invisible – to touch everything with your eyes without being touched back?

We decided to push on to Mount Rushmore, backwards in time from Spielberg to Hitchcock, while the weather held. Driving from the sci-fi specter towards the histrionic immensity of those stone reliefs, we felt the giddiness of entering an image that had previously lacked depth. It was as if Wiley E. Coyote had drawn a tunnel into the mountainside and we had driven through.

Back on the highway, the sky remained flawless. But as we started up into the Black Hills a tremendous fog descended, spreading and thickening around the landscape. We pressed on, convinced that the gloom would pass, just in time, in the spirit of the day's sudden and miraculous clarity.

The mist, though, only deepened: a milky swirl growing ever more opaque, until it curdled nearly solid in the air. The reach of our vision collapsed to about 20 feet, and the sparse traffic slowed to a bewildered crawl. By the time we reached the national park, it was impossible to see more than 15 feet in any direction. The entrance rose up against the fog with all the gothic menace of a ghostly mansion. We rolled up to a booth, and were greeted by a sympathetically smiling square-jawed park ranger. With unexpected anxiety in my voice, I began to speak: "Is the park open?"

"Yes," he said, "it is. But you cannot see the monument at all."

"So, is admission free?" I dared.

"No, I'm sorry. It's not. But can I give a treat to your dog?"

"That would be great."

And through the crack in a slobber-streaked window, reflecting nothing but fog, the hound received his biscuit. There was merriment, but no resolution. The ranger offered to let us drive in to circle around and exit through the parking lot. We had come this far. Something would redeem us.

In the middle of the desolate lot, I parked the car. I opened the trunk and pulled out my tripod, erecting it on the asphalt. I loaded my film, mounted the camera and took in the impenetrable enclosure of mist. Assessing the scene, I estimated the presence of the monumental carved faces in front of me. I adjusted the height, leveled the device, focused on the furthest visible object in the frame, and took a picture towards Mount Rushmore. At least I knew that it was in there.

The next morning, in the lowlands, the sun was again brilliant. We drove back into the hills, and this time, the clarity held. The new ranger had no twinkle, and certainly no biscuits, and the parking lot was already half full. I parked again in the same space, opened the trunk, and set up my camera and tripod where I remembered placing them before. Settling in at the same height, in the same direction, I waited a minute for a lull in passing cars and ambling tourists. Then, with the sun to my side and those great stone portraits completely to my back, I framed and shot the same scene that I had documented the day before: a vista of approaching clouds opening past the tarmac, with an infinity of indefinite wilderness beyond.

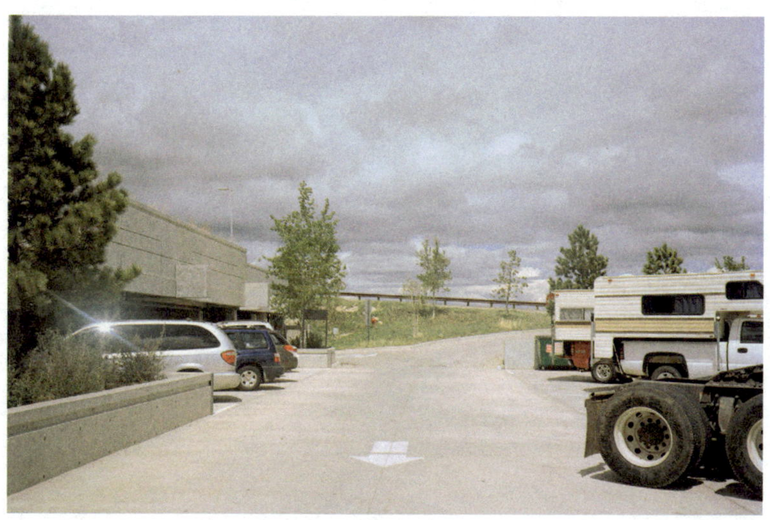

Mountain Shadow Place was commissioned for and published in *The Andrew Project: 1000 and Something Portraits in Toronto, Berlin and London, 2010-2013* by Shaan Tariq Hassan-Syed, (London: S1 Artspace and Form Content, 2013). It was first released in a limited-edition book as *Mountain Shadow Place* by Nicholas Muellner, (Ithaca, NY: A-Jump Books, 2012).

VIX.

The New Interval

Invented and used by earthlings, the photograph is the stuff of
extraterrestrials.
      —Henri Van Lier, *Philosophy of Photography* (1981)

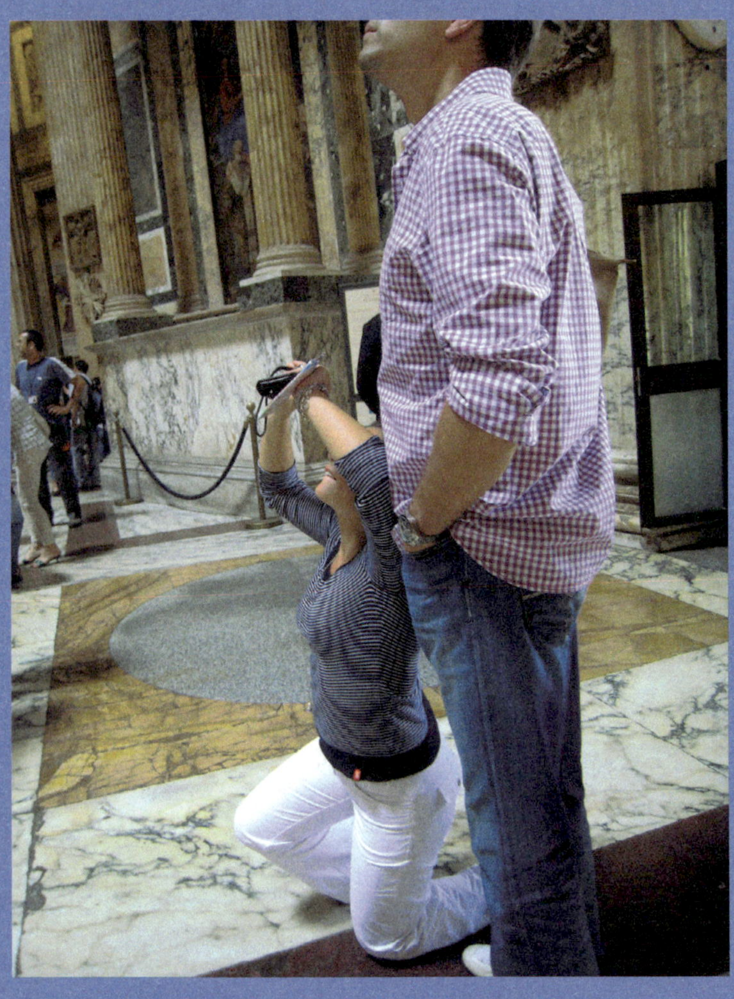

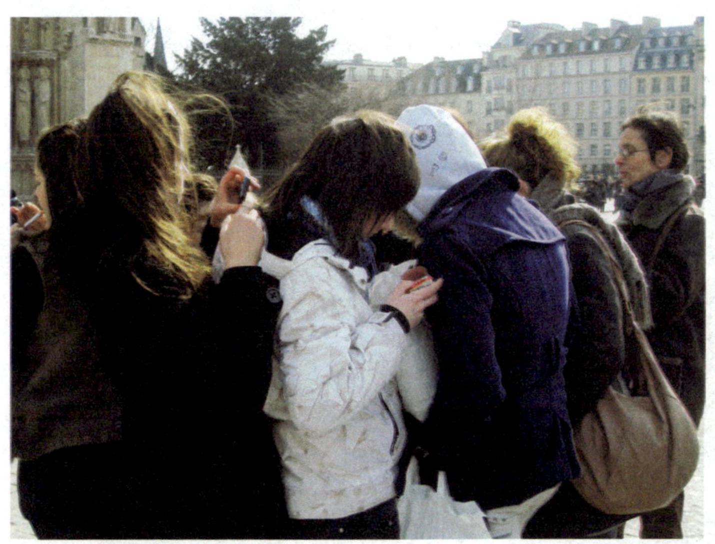

I. The New Interval

AT FIRST IT WAS SIMPLY a fascination with the pose: the awkward gesture of holding a camera up to the space *in front of* one's face. These 4 to 15 inches, between the photographer's nose and the screen of a digital camera, constitute a new interval in the world – a space that demands further investigation.

I do not subscribe to apocalyptic or utopian readings of the paradigm shifts enacted by the digitization of photography. After all, pictures are still pictures – flat and mute – and we still use cameras to take them. But the vernacular experience of photographing *feels* different and that is because a new space, between eyes and screens, has opened up, while another quite different gap has closed. The old experience was charged with the occult darkness of the film chamber; the new one is flooded with the brightness of the open field. These two encounters produce very different relationships to the creation of the image. In the new space of photography, a picture impresses itself upon us before we make it; in the old order, we impressed the image upon ourselves before we knew it.

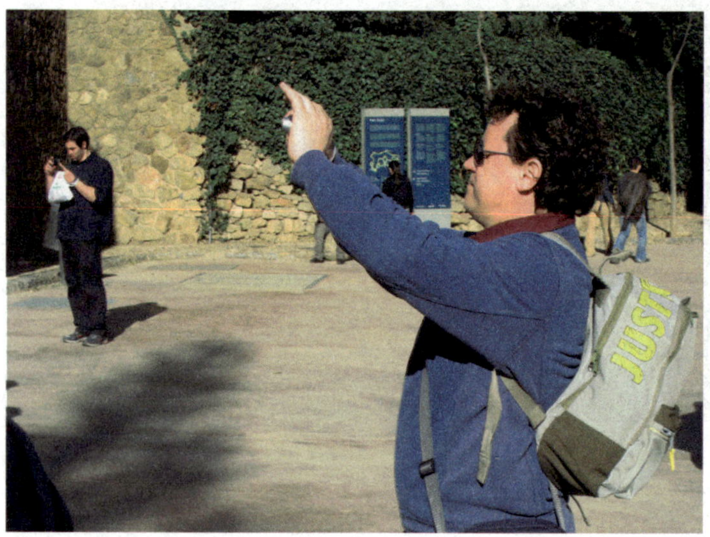

Over the past five years I have spent a great deal of time watching people *view* the pictures they were taking. I came to suspect that while the simultaneity of digital photography had relieved some of the ontological uncertainty of the old medium, a new difficulty had been created. Now, the body is apparent – planted before the subject – but the mind seems elsewhere. I observed photographers' slack-jawed attitudes and intense, yet absent, stares turned rapturously on their tiny camera screens, and I wanted to know: *Where are they?*

Belgian philosopher Henri Van Lier's *Philosophy of Photography* was written in 1981, but was not widely available in print until 2005 (and not in English until 2007). He died in 2009, and although he lived to see and write elsewhere about the digital age, this text is something of a Rip Van Winkle – recently awoken into a changed world. Despite, or perhaps because of this temporal blind spot, I found myself drawn to its trippy, sometimes spellbound affect when watching people take pictures. Van Lier both scolded and valorized analog photography for the thicket of formal and empirical contingencies in which the making and viewing of pictures was constantly entangled. For him, much of this indeterminacy was born in the dark space of the interval between exposing the negative and being exposed to the image. This is precisely the space that has disappeared in the current experience of digital-camera photography – shifting the act from a ritual of hope carried out across darkness, toward a process of assessment and dissemination grounded in luminous clarity.

Van Lier's text is as much a philosophy *through* photography as *for* photography, and its existential thrust hinges on the terror of the real lurking behind the flimsy picture plane of our reality. Or, as he puts it: "In the encounter of photons and halides, the real engenders the black spots while the reality intimates that these are indeed marks and zones." Photography both obscures and reveals our desperate mental game in ways that words cannot.

He refused to address photography in the language of semiotics, insisting that "the slightest excess of vocabulary would be fatal . . . because it threatens to obfuscate what is most specific to the photographic index, namely its *terrible* muteness, which one is in danger of confusing with the eloquence of signs."

In Van Lier's oracular world, "the photographer inhabits the *camera obscura*, and he ultimately and always draws in the future viewers with him." I hold a picture in my hands knowing that I am reading it across a dark passage of temporal loss and limited signification. In the old analog order of photography, this sensation of viewing inevitably infected the experience of photographing. With the camera to my eye, I already sensed that the image was going to be *other* – an alien offspring of the moment

I shared with the shutter mechanism. I was there, but my picture would always be elsewhere: "What is most important for photography — as with interstellar space — is the night . . . the darkness and non-light out of which luminous eventualities manifest themselves punctually and incidentally, emerging out of the dark only to return to it."

What, then, becomes of Van Lier's black hole in the digital age, when the image is in front of us before we are ever alone with either our sensations or our hopes? What future are we imagining for our pictures now, and how does that shift our photographing moment?

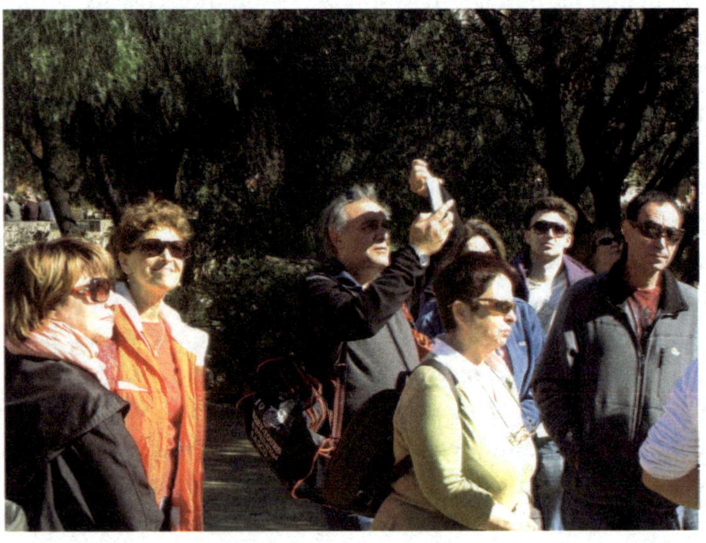

Today, most people see the image before they "shoot" it — already a flattened, bright rectangle — rather than a peephole promise of what will most likely be a photograph. Furthermore, the contingency of what Van Lier calls "indices and indexes" — of what will appear and what it may mean — is given over to instantaneous assessment. The photograph is immediately evaluated in terms of the still-present scene and subject. We take pictures. We examine them, perhaps glancing at the subject as a helpful reference. We edit and repeat the process in an effort at refinement or accuracy – perhaps in a further stab at attractiveness and spontaneity. And then we do it all again.

One could imagine that this new simultaneity would relieve the disturbingly "contingent" experience of the old medium. But it seems instead to have shifted the burden. With analog photography, we always knew that no matter how much we tried to control the outcome and imagine the future image, the picture was uncertain in a way that we were not. We saw the world before the photograph reconstituted it for us. That, at least, is how it seemed. In other words, the analog photograph betrayed its own instability so we didn't have to question ours. Twentieth-century theorists' perpetual degrading of the medium's "truth content" was merely an attempt to reassure ourselves that we were made of more solid stuff. But the jig, as they say, is up. The digital camera inverts this paradigm. The future is no longer a question of what the picture will be. *What we will be* in front of the picture is the new contingency of photography.

What, exactly, does this future promise? In an optimistic mood, I like to think of it as a ritual of enacting presence in the teeth of the experiential collapse demanded by incessant consumerism. In the newly extended moment of the photograph (viewing, shooting, editing, viewing, shooting, editing) we shop for the image that will buy us the best future moment of visual consumption. We edit our camera pictures the same way we shop for sneakers online – looking at a picture and imagining our future with it. It is both a deeper submission to consumerism and a more ardent resistance to alienation than photography has previously encompassed. Increasingly, the ritual of viewing photographs is no longer about forging a tenuous connection to the past – or even about memory. It is, rather, an act of repeatedly reconstituting a presence that feels situated in time, resonating between a past and a future that suggests the now, while constantly deferring it. The picture is always present, even before it is fixed. We are the ones who have come unmoored.

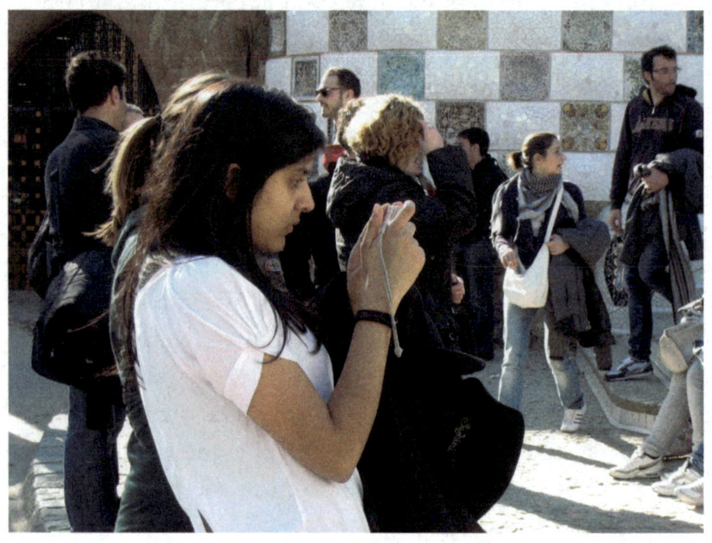

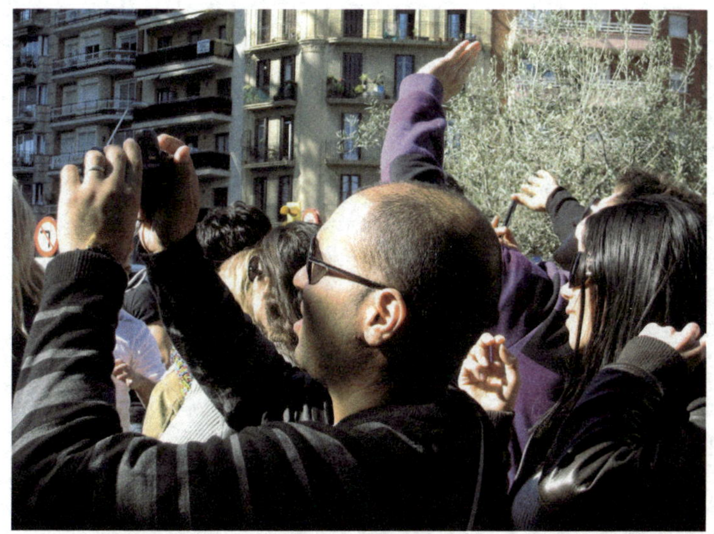

II. The Huddle

"One usually chatters around a photograph, when passing the family album around for instance, in order to simultaneously dispel the panic of the real lurking underneath and in order to animate a feeble reality."

Watching people participate in the immediate collective viewing of digital camera pictures does not dispel Van Lier's ontologically desperate reading of the social exchange around photographs in the analog age. But just because we're fighting off panic doesn't mean we're not, momentarily, succeeding. These acts of urgent huddling – the couple photographs each other and reviews the results; friends gather around a cell phone to admire *what has just happened* – provides a reassurance of shared presence. In doing so, it momentarily recharges the promise implied but deferred in the moment of picture-taking. It is precisely this social performance that we hope to reanimate in our future encounter with the already familiar image, huddling again around the device that is both camera and album, or imagining the intimate collective of buddies, remotely huddled around our recent uploads.

An observation: Last spring I watched a tall young man take self-portraits in front of a church. He placed himself between his camera and the landmark, holding the device down and out at arm's length. He exposed some pictures and pirouetted quickly to evaluate them in reference to the building behind him, now placing the screen between himself and the scene. He held the camera down, using his body to block the sun's glare as he backed into a passerby. Later, in the photograph, he will be present. But, I thought, he is not here now. The picture is already exactly itself, and he is the one lost in space.

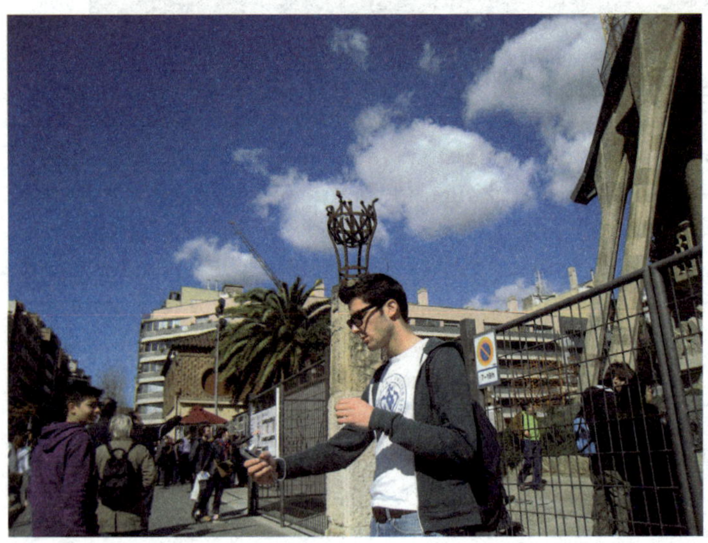

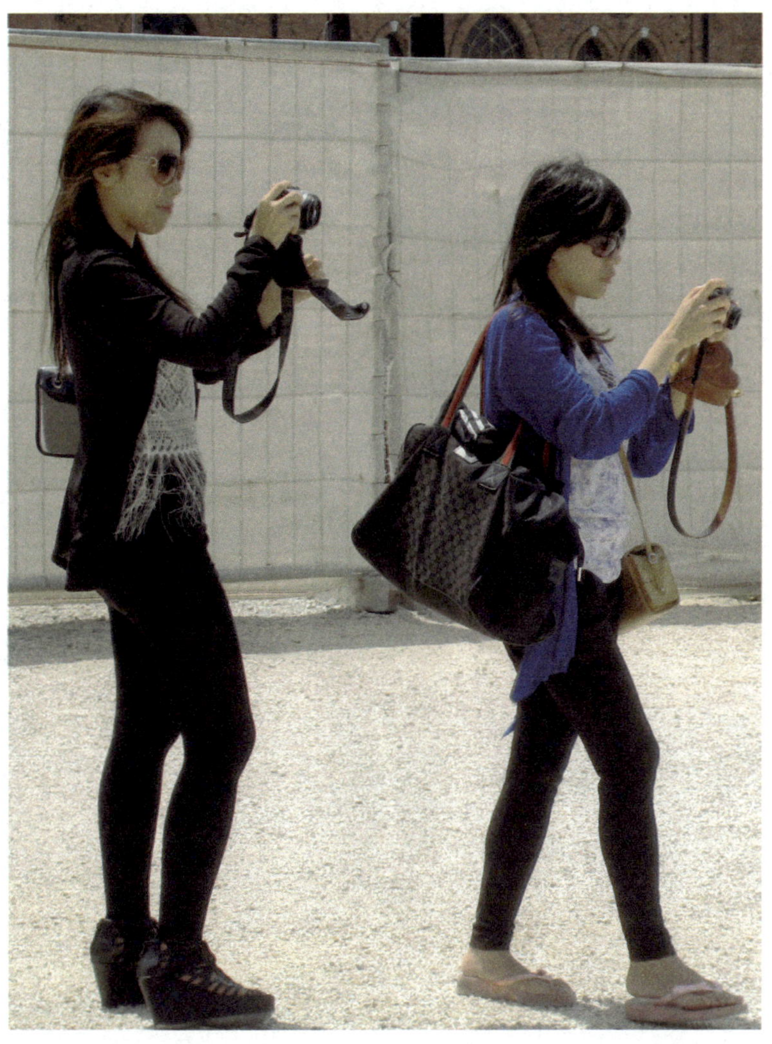

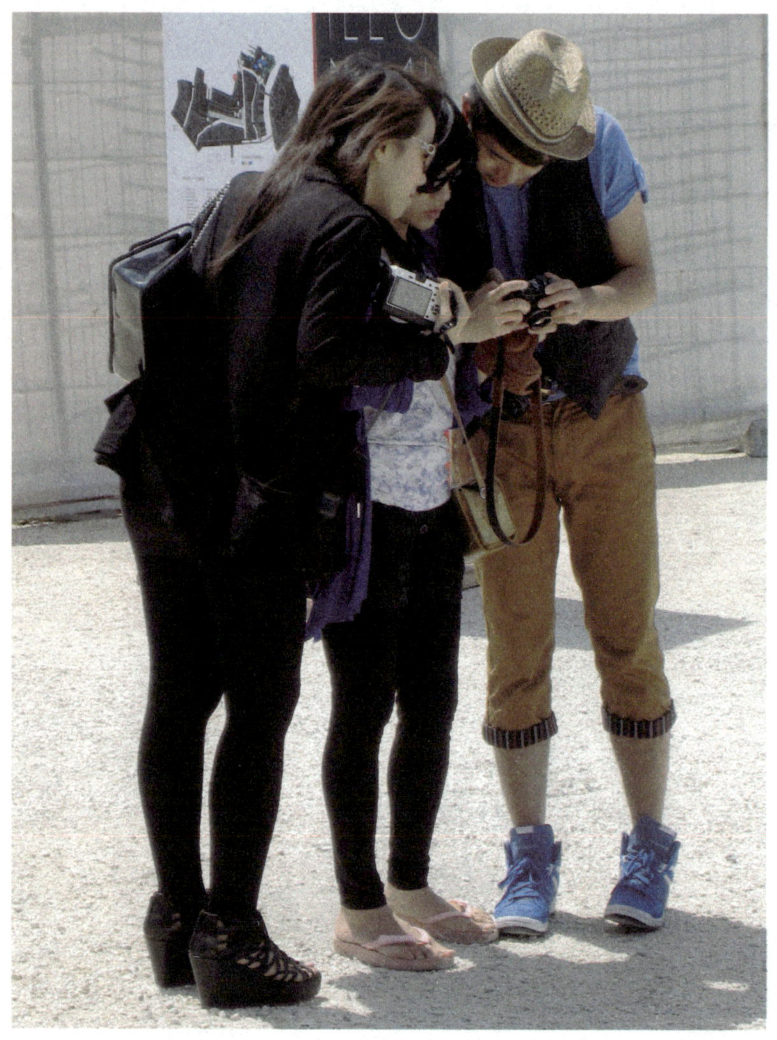

III. The Serpent

In one of his more freewheeling passages, Van Lier compares the analog photograph – as an object that habitually escapes "interpretation and decoding" – to a serpent: "The fascinating serpent transfixes us through its movement from back to front (the intervals of the negative of the negative), and left to right (the lateral overlap of indices)." The indeterminate movement of "reading" across the picture plane still remains, but Van Lier's oscillation of negatives and positives – a temporal movement between the *then* of the exposure and the *now* of the print – has disappeared in contemporary photography. It has been replaced by another temporal fluttering: between the immediately visible photograph and the future economy of the image. Furthermore, in the taking of digital photos we are confronted with the simultaneous appearance of the picture and its subject: a pair of indivisible but irreconcilable appearances.

Van Lier contends that "the serpent is not actually perceived by the one who is fascinated and stunned by it." To the extent that photographers imagine the picture's future reception while absently scanning its instantaneous appearance, this observation is precisely true. To Van Lier, the photograph/serpent "establishes a non-space and non-duration, outside of the imaginary" as a function of its delayed appearance and syntactical indeterminacy. The digital-camera image, no less indeterminate, but infinitely more immediate, recasts this logic. In the extended moment of picture-making and picture-viewing, we alternately confront the physical subject (person, place, thing) and the quite distinct vessel of ideas and narratives (what Van Lier calls "mental schemas") that the photograph inevitably becomes. As with all ecstatic rituals, we demand presence but cannot be present. The picture holds its ground while the photographer drifts off into a spatiotemporal

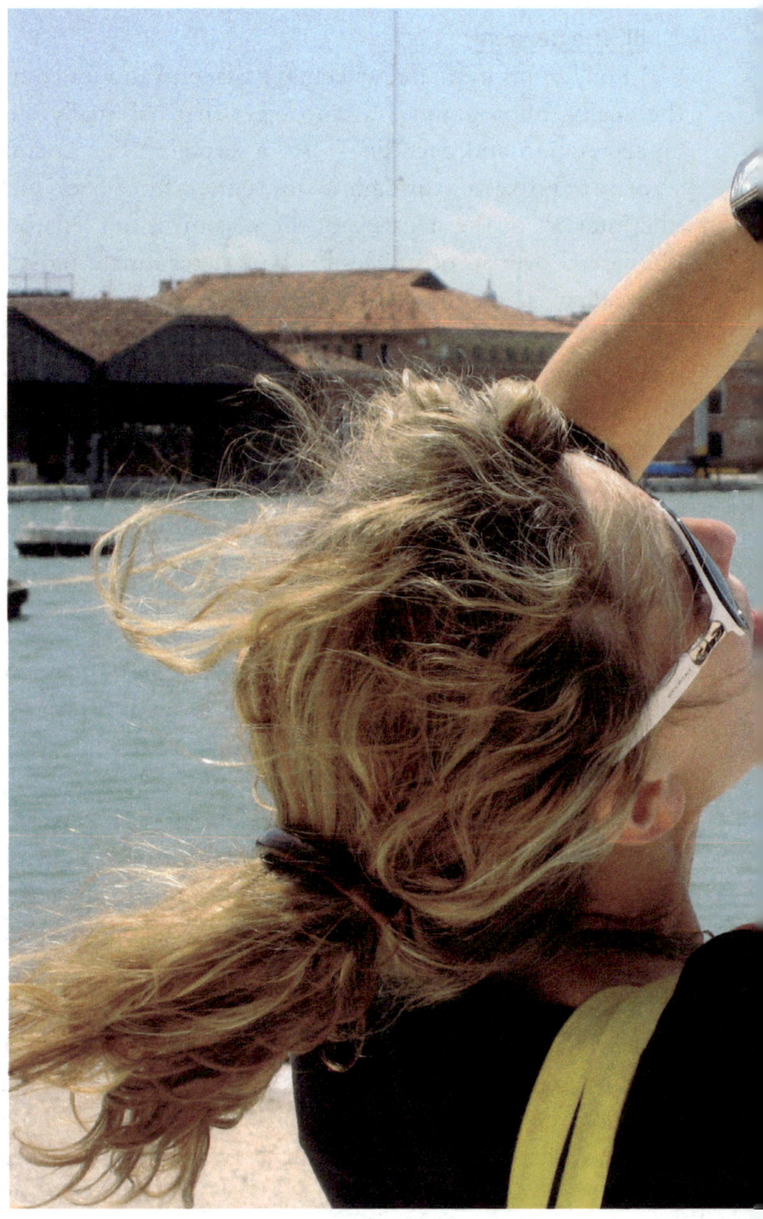

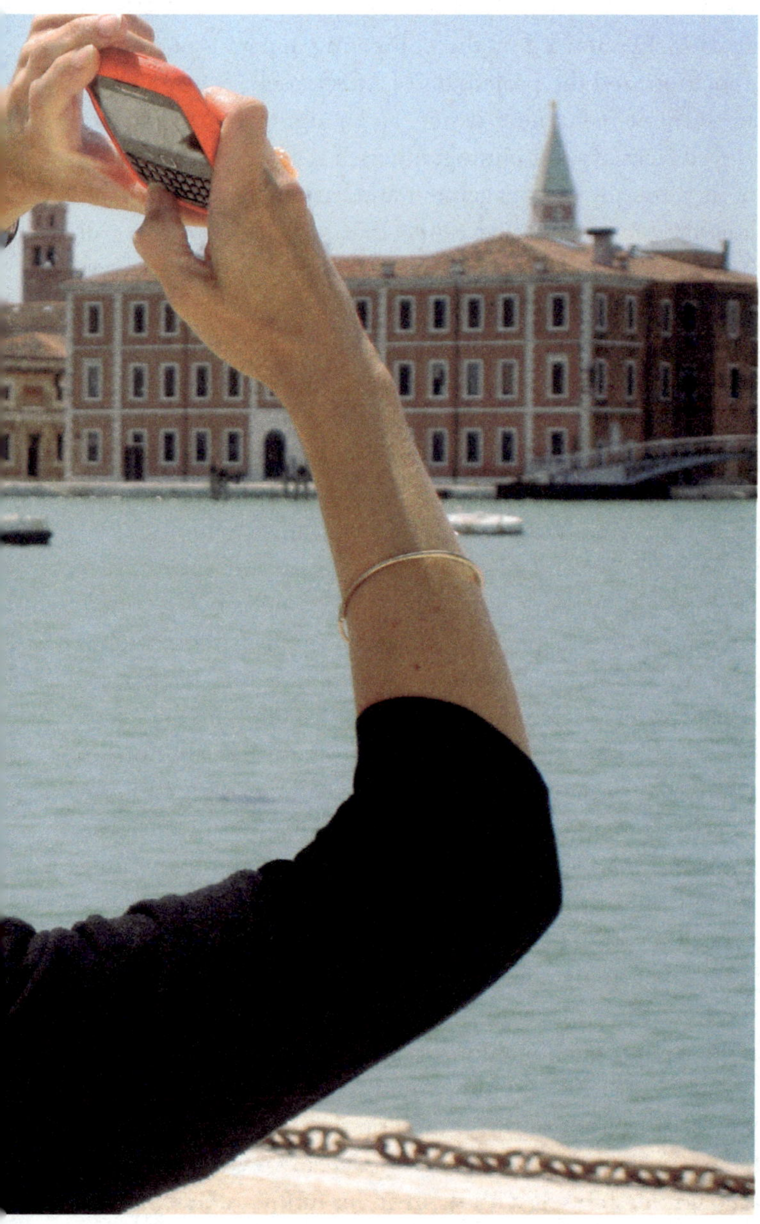

netherworld, hypnotized by the competing demands of reading, representation, and the projection of a future self.

The serpent has a new dance, and judging by the gaping, glassy-eyed faces of most photographers, it is seductive. We could assume it is the joy of engagement and mastery: *I am here; I am taking pictures; I am analyzing, editing, and enjoying them!* After all, the rhetoric of this new media is all about our immediate ownership of experience, and the voice or vision that we can broadcast in affirmation of that achievement. But I suspect that the sensation is closer to weightlessness than anything else. We are already thinking about where we will send or post our images; about how they will be captioned and who will be impressed or entertained. What passes for the joy of presence is really the vertiginous freefall of alienation. We are expressed as a future commodity of the self, registering and recalibrating at electronic speeds. It is exhilarating and hypnotic, but it is not the same as being there.

Something does happen to us in the thrall of those inches between our eyes and our screens. Our sleek little imaging devices evoke another era's science fiction while signaling this era's baseline of social participation. Even so, when we push the button we are transported, or perhaps exported, before the image is ever sent. We experience *ekstasis*, in the true sense of being outside ourselves.

I looked at the LCD image of the young man photographing himself in front of the church. I took some pictures. I reviewed them, but they didn't seem to explain the queerness of what I had seen — that strange disassociation of self from context, in the very gesture of trying to affirm just that. How could I tell you about this strange phenomenon, of the man doubling himself and disappearing all at once? How would I explain that he was not really present in front of the church on that lovely spring day? I wanted to try again, but by then he was already reviewing his pictures, imagining himself with them, in his future, as he staggered away. He was right in front of me, but he was no longer there. And neither was I.

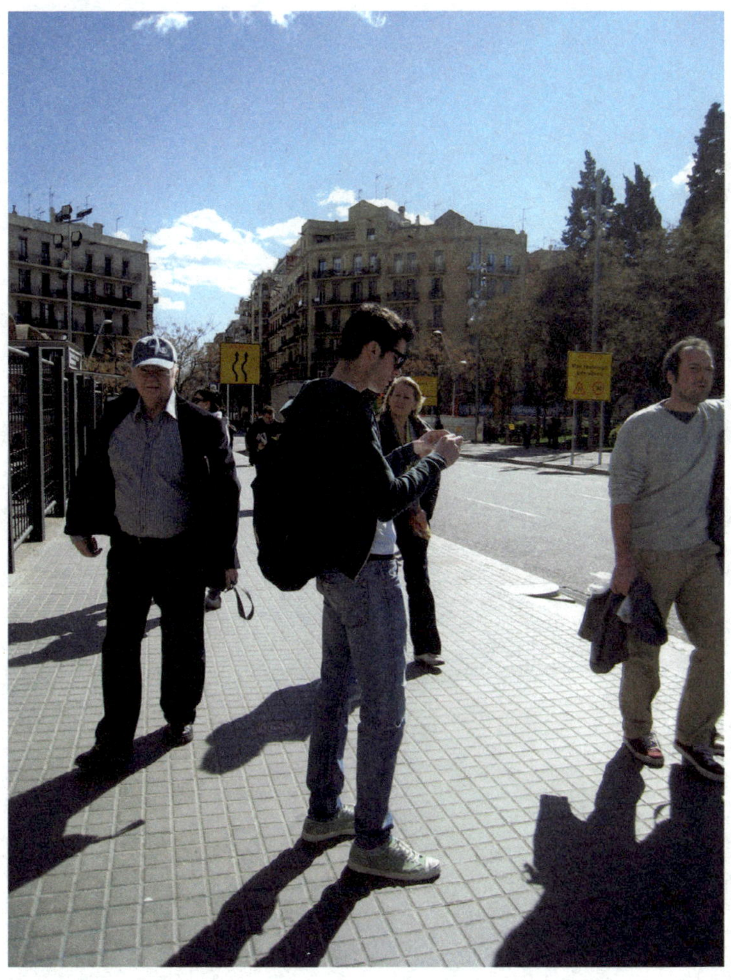

Earlier versions of "The New Interval" were published in *The Versatile Image: Photography in the Era of Web 2.0.*, edited by Alexandra Moschovi (Leuven: Leuven University Press, 2013) and in *Afterimage*, edited by Karen vanMeenen, *38*:6 (May/June, 2011).

X.

The Parable of the Jackass

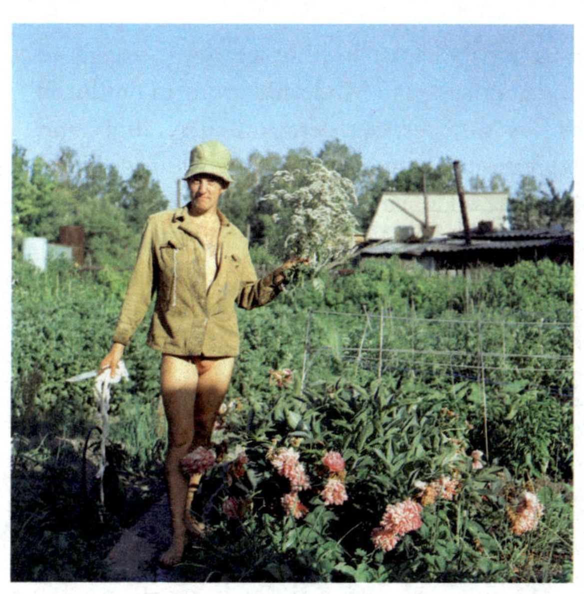

IN 1990, I HAD THE GOOD FORTUNE to find myself traveling alone with two cameras, across the entire eastern expanse of the collapsing Soviet Union. To my 20-year-old eyes, the streets and people of Siberia seemed like an exotic storehouse of late-modernist photographic forms: William Klein's arrangements of bodies; Garry Winogrand's kinetic formal jokes; Helen Levitt's vocabulary of languid gesture and innocent violence; Diane Arbus's stares. In Siberia, in 1990, I also found a young man named Alyosha, and probably fell in love with him, but that love, then, was a form I could not read.

In 2009, just after my 40th birthday, I returned to the Russian Far East, determined to find that no-longer-young Alyosha. Hiking back and forth across Ulan-Ude, his provincial hometown near the Mongolian border, I found myself preoccupied by a decidedly different moment in photography's history: the rise and fall of the American Pictorialist movement at the turn of the 20th century.

That awkward transitional chapter in photography's struggle to pass from Victorian handmaiden to Modernist art form produced a catalogue of brushy surfaces, overdetermined symbols, and aching, earnest expressionistic figures. It was a curious complex of the domestic and the allegorical, featuring outsized physical gestures of tenderness, longing, dignity and vague spiritual suggestion. Nothing about the visible nature of Ulan-Ude evoked the iconography of this crucial and largely discarded photographic moment, and I struggled to make sense of the connection. In the process, I developed an argument. Under the circumstances, I would like to call it a parable.

The problem of fitting photography successfully and clearly into the trajectory of Modernism stems from the difficulty of separating out the actual/factual/material from that which is projected/desired/imagined. In other words, it is hard to say when we are dealing in "subjects" and when we are dealing in imaginary projection, or what the literary critics once called "pathetic fallacy." With a photograph, it seems, we are always dealing with both, while for most of the 20th century we pretended that we were only dealing in "subjects."

And let's say, for the moment, that the 19th-century English critic John Ruskin is to blame, in part because great rhetoricians are always fun to scapegoat, and in larger part because his influence was so broadly felt in the transition from Victorian sentiment to Modernist asceticism. The material fact of his influence was brought home to me on a bus to a 19th-century psychiatric hospital in south London. In one short journey I passed Ruskin Way, Ruskin Close, Ruskin Walk: the road to madness was paved with Ruskin. And like the photographer Alfred Stieglitz in his wake, he was a Romantic sensualist with a clinician's icy mind — bent on redefining art's terms so as to pull the rug out from under his aesthete contemporaries.

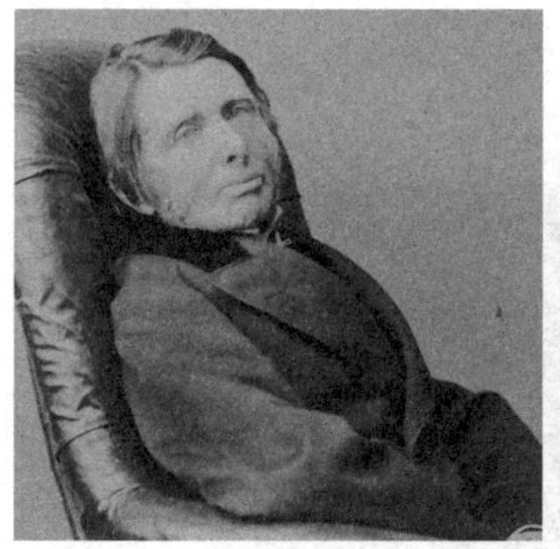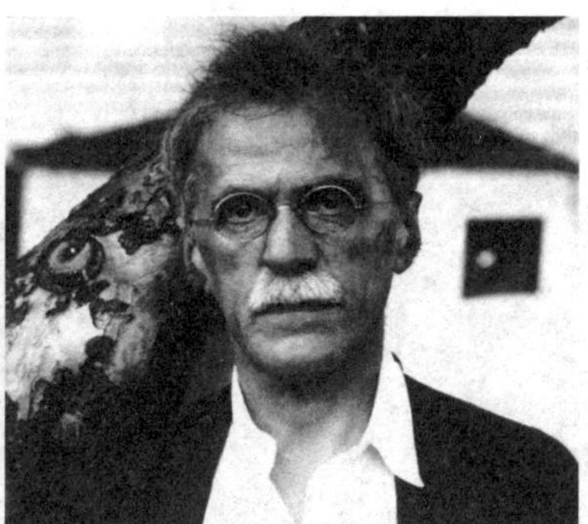

Would you trust these men with your medium?

Ruskin dug a ditch for photography while elevating painting to the level of poetry. In a number of essays, most famously, "Of the Pathetic Fallacy" (1856), Ruskin argued that, despite his adherence to the principle of truth, the most powerful works of art succeed through "false" metaphor and inaccurate descriptive invention. Great artists, he asserts, "are yet submitted to influences stronger than they, and see in a sort untruly, because what they see is inconceivably above them. This last is the usual condition of prophetic inspiration." Artists turn to fallacy in their role as cultural mediums, translating the intensity of their rare insights into a language "broken, obscure, and wild in metaphor, resembling that of the weaker man, overborne by weaker things." The rest of us cannot see what they see, but art can produce the sensation of that impression within us.

The power of fallacy that Ruskin thus delineates is dependent on a discourse of emergence. The reader creates the image in her imagination, and it is through this coextensive experience that the poet's expression of longing for what is "untrue" becomes the reader's own. We can immediately imagine how this works in literature, where the author is our guide to the images we must finish in our own heads. It also translates easily to painting, through the artist's authority to suggest synthetic perceptions in a plastic language of pure invention.

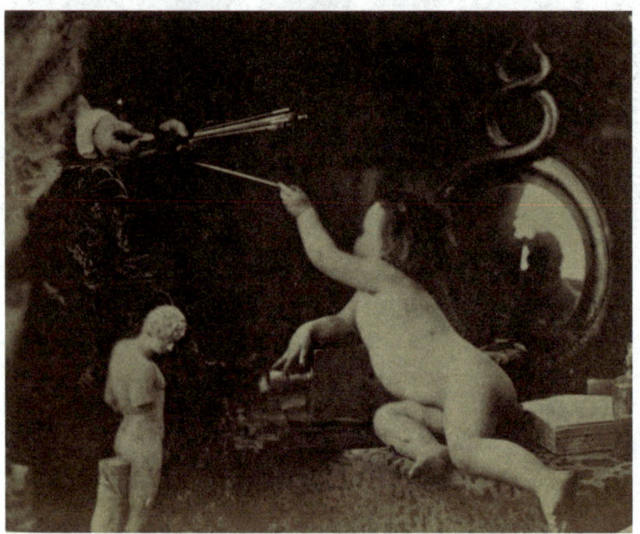

But the poor infant robot photography is nowhere in this picture. It is a medium, but never a Medium. The image is always a message or a description, but never a means of transubstantiation. Its fundamental grounding in authorless factuality allows it to be a liar, or a failure, but never a prophet of the unrepresentable.

The photograph suggests, by habit and learning, that it is already read for us. It feels manifest and not emergent. Ruskin urged landscape painters to be faithful to a "true impression" of the scene rather than to accurate description. Thus, the otherwise incommunicable encounter with place would be born anew in the spectator's encounter with the artwork. One can easily view the desperate contortions of Pictorialist photography as a vain attempt to arrive at the painter or poet's vocabulary of emergence and impression.

In the 1910s, Alfred Stieglitz promoted an ingenious compromise that would smuggle photography into the ranks of modern art. An image-making and image-reading regime that proposed a kind of perpetual double vision: the seemingly forthright move towards the "straight" photograph. The image served, immediately, to describe a subject, free from fallacy, fancy or obfuscation. But the image also enabled, through gesture, form, and indeterminate but suggestive content, the allegedly free flight of a viewer's imagination. The spectator saw the subject as it was, but she could also see another subject, the transcendent subject, as it emerged in her active consciousness. This sleight of hand was both a trick of cultural positioning and a specific campaign of image-making that encouraged such a "reading" experience. The modern viewing audience was invited to seduce these austere and flirtatious pictures in the company of Braque, Matisse and Brancusi – in other words, in the context of difficult and abstract art that clearly rewarded the active labor of the elite viewer. Stieglitz was busy sealing this new deal at the very moment he was aggressively dismantling the cultural influence of Pictorialism, the movement he had previously championed.

Take, for example, the following two images: Anne Brigman's circa-1910 Pictorialist work *Finis* and Alfred Stieglitz's 1922 Modernist work *Portrait of Georgia Engelhard*. The titles alone begin to tell the story. The desire for meaning – metaphorical, emotional – in the Brigman image is so strong as to precede both the reading of the subject and the reading of metaphor. The coercion towards interpretation – the blasted tree, the contorted figure, the dramatically treated areas of tone and surface – precludes the spectator's capacity to let meaning or feeling emerge "of its own accord" in the imagination. This interference is heightened by the viewer's knowledge that there was, ultimately, a naked woman next to a tree, and that we are being fairly begged to interpret her and her woody companion as doubled icons of anguish, loss and isolation. The photographer wants viewers to read manifest assertion as emergent meaning. Fat chance.

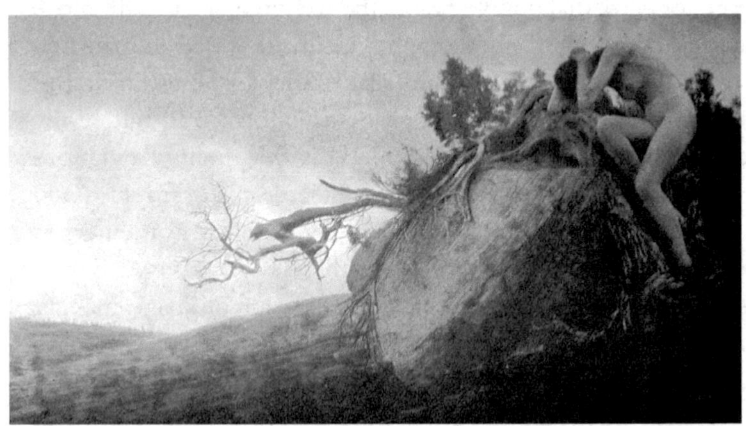

Stieglitz's photograph, meanwhile, reads quite differently. His naturalization of the allegorical is what leaves room for our mental "intervention," or so it feels. Though we don't believe in the image as factual reportage, we do believe in the subject's presence in a determinate time and space, and not simply as a compositional element of allegorical construction. We immediately read the figure and her situation within a discourse of descriptive realism – the hang of her breasts, the tactile prospect of her naked ass on the coarse wood frame, her tenuous hold on that armful of apples. But we also can, if we so choose, move into the realm of meaning – about transition, time, erotic youth and fruity fertility. All of that reading, though, is on us. The artist did not tell us to do this; he only made the movement of idea and interpretation possible – or this, at least, is how we feel it, and this is Stieglitz's diabolical trick. The crux here is not so much what Allan Sekula, speaking of Stieglitz, once described as "the semantic autonomy of the photograph," but its implicit corollary: the illusion of the viewer's interpretive autonomy.

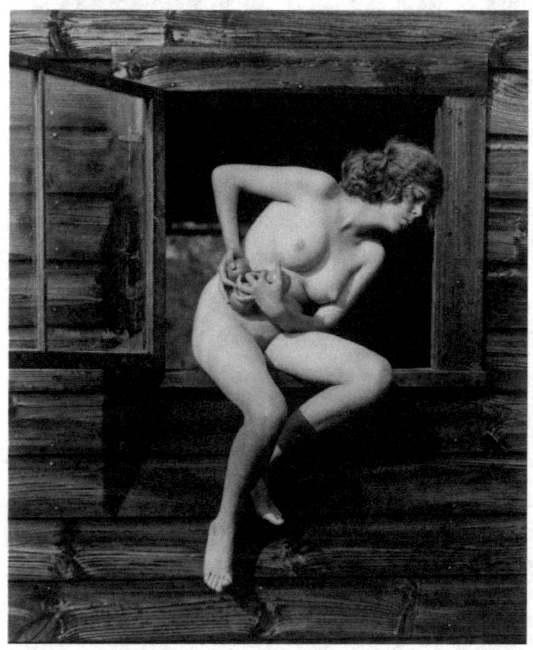

In recent years, I had been unable to figure out why this modernist maneuver — a structure that has overshadowed the trajectory of art photography for almost the past century — had become so annoying to me. And I was also unable to understand why, exactly, I kept thinking about Gertrude Käsebier and the desperate overdetermination of Pictorialist style, while I wandered around Ulan-Ude, searching in vain and taking pictures. I kept thinking it had to do with broken and blasted trees, and I photographed accordingly. But it was only months later, editing and assembling all of my pictures, that an unanticipated slide comparison threw the whole endeavor into a clearer relief.

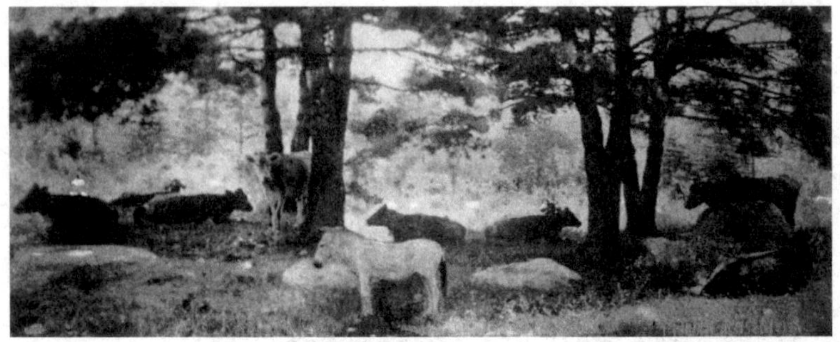

The first image – bearing, for my money, one of the best titles in the entire history of photography – is Käsebier's undated (circa 1900) photograph, *The Pathos of the Jackass*. Certainly this picture, and its profoundly instructive title, tells us much about the desperation for meaning that characterizes the doomed Pictorialist project. But the second image, also of some form of diminutive equine character, put a finer point on things. It is a photograph that I made through a cake-shop window, across the street from Ulan-Ude's main department store. We see, through a haze of glass reflection, a somewhat misshapen toy pony. And where the bright reflection gives way to a clearer window on our subject, we can read the urgent inscription, composed in English for our clearer understanding: I LOVE U.

The Pictorialist subject is, explicitly, a desirous subject. It wants to be wanted, and it wants to mean something more to you. This is the vulnerability – and availability – denied to the Modernist photographic subject almost all of the time, from Stieglitz to Frank to Friedlander and beyond.

The photograph says: *I want you to know this! I need you to understand!* And as any gal on a first date knows, that message is a losing gambit.

It is not lost on me that a straight man invented photographic Modernism as a tool to murder a movement rife with women

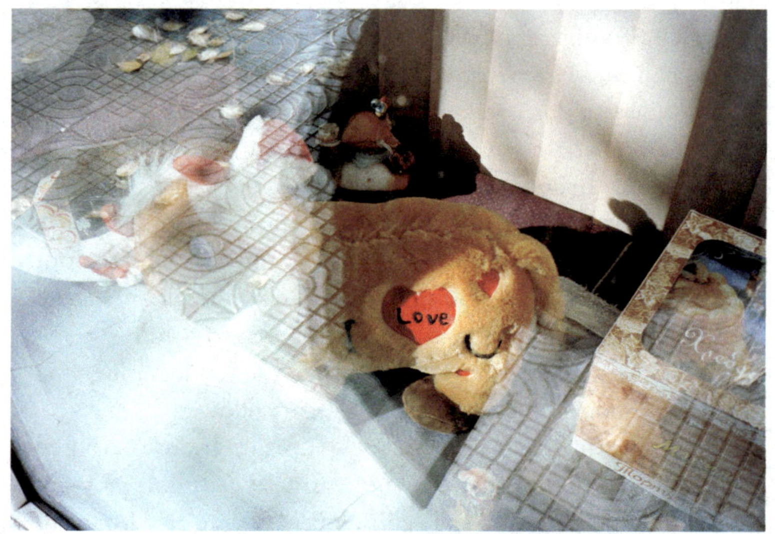

and gay men. At the height of her success, Käsebier was perhaps the most popular fine-art photographer in the United States, and important Pictorialist exhibitions always included significant representations of women, beyond what most contemporary museum exhibitions would even aspire to. Pictorialism also elevated the spiritualist queerness of F. Holland Day, as well as the extravagance of the self-ennobled Baron de Meyer, whose melodramatic aesthetic set the terms for the first decades of American fashion photography.

The aesthetic and metaphorical scrims of the Pictorialist project carved spaces for marginal desires to become passionately readable shapes outside the masculine canon of modern art. The everyday fabric and emotional needs of women's lives, as well as female and same-sex longing, were woven into the gauzy, layered folds of Pictorialism, and I can't help but feel that only a straight white man would have the unfettered confidence to invent an art that claimed to lay everything out on the table, without offering an ounce of vulnerability. Only men like Stieglitz and Weston could say: *Look! Here, so elegantly exposed, is the ass I plan to grab! I will not tell you what it signifies, but formal authority means truth.* Who needs longing when you can have it both ways?

Sure, Anne Brigman had to add a broken tree to talk seriously about a woman's desire and disappointment, and F. Holland Day had to dress up his hot young men as scantily clad centurions guarding the crucified Christ (modeled by Day himself). But these tropes allowed their erotic and psychic dramas to be directly felt and seen. Stieglitz's Modernism banished the tender smuggling of sincere emotion that Pictorialist allegory allowed.

Returning to Siberia after nearly two decades, I was confronted with the memory of that closeted early 1990s photographer; the one of the painfully split consciousness who tried hard to embrace the measured disavowal of need (one might call it the formal acrobatics of repression) that, as a photographer, I had been reared on. But in 2009, I was no longer willing or able to make pictures that participated in the willful separation of desire from expression – that embraced the mannered dissociation from self that Stieglitz's devil's bargain with Ruskin's ghost required. In this orthodoxy, the photograph had to pretend not to care (too much) and the viewer had to pretend not to know (or notice) that the image cares. I wanted to make pictures that communicated, unmeasured, their needs and messages. Yet I did not know how. Furthermore, the objects of my fascination and desire – Alyosha, his friends, the picturesque swoon of late-Soviet society – they had vanished. I was not a medium, and I had no metaphors. What, then, was I doing there, a donkey among alien cows? Such is the pathos of the jackass.

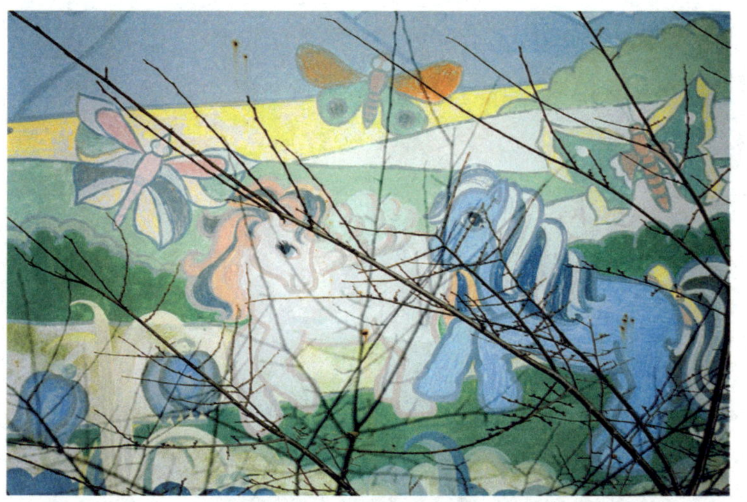

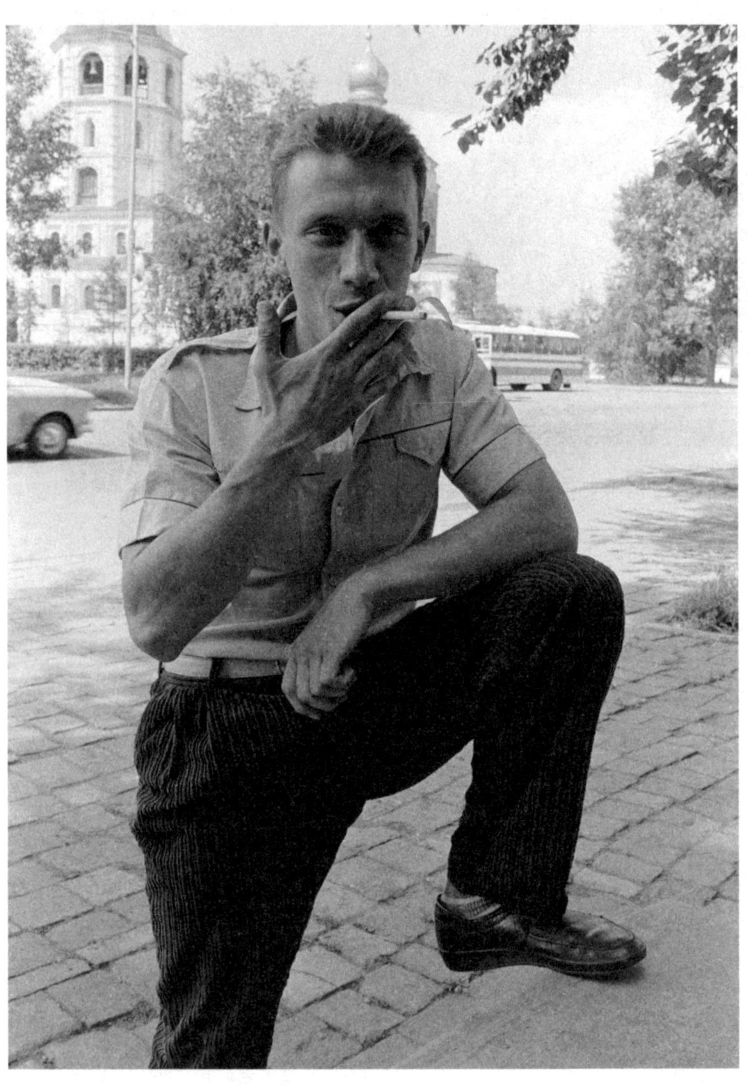

An earlier version of this text was published in *The Amnesia Pavilions* by Nicholas Muellner, (Ithaca, NY: A-Jump Books, 2011).

XI.

The Photograph Commands Indifference

I LIVE IN THE TOWN of West Danby, in Tompkins County, NY. My official mailing address is Spencer, a village eight miles south, in Tioga County. I pay municipal taxes to Danby, the town over the hills to the east. My school taxes go to Van Etten, over another set of hills to the southwest. A Newfield-based company called Superior picks up my garbage. One Mrs. James Casterline apparently owns the water system and I pay her directly. The town has large, new, carved wooden signs marking its beginning and end as you drive north or south on Route 34. Route 34 is also Route 96 during that stretch, and depending on where you're standing on the road and which way you're thinking of going, it may alternately be referred to as Spencer Road or Newfield Road. The space bounded by the town's signs contains no shops, businesses or public spaces. At the midpoint between the signs is a small, picturesque white clapboard church structure, which is not actually a church anymore, but a modern events center used by urbanites for out-of-town gatherings: meetings, reunions, perhaps weddings. Except for the facts of its framing and naming as a place, West Danby does not speak for itself at all. In this, the town is like a photograph.

Introduction

Of all the economies in the world that are fed by cheap raw materials, there is perhaps none so glutted with resources as the economy of metaphor. Every *thing*, when you think about it, is just waiting to have meaning assigned to or discovered in it. And one task that most things do well – in addition to whatever worldly function they may serve – is waiting. Objects in the world are quite stoical in this regard. They bear it with equanimity, if not indifference. I sometimes imagine they wish it would not happen to them. It's not the honor you might think.

There are, of course, certain classes of objects that have the arrogance or misfortune (you can already tell this is our fault) to assert meaning: to demand reading, empathy, investment and elevation. This includes artworks of course, with their metastasizing apparatuses of rationalizing discourses, histories, markets, institutions and aesthetics. But more to the point, there are monuments. Monuments try the hardest and are given the least help. They are outposts and desperate cartoons of the metaphorical economy of thing-meaning. Abandoned in squares, on corners, in parks and courtyards, they are so little trusted to convey their intention that it is usually inscribed on them somewhere, like children's names on summer-camp clothing. They require metaphor ID in the likely event that their meaning is misplaced along the way. The terrible thing about monuments is that they yearn so terribly to mean something; they mean so very much to say something, but inert mass and silence are their only absolute assets. If the distant god of the Romantics, disinterested almost to the point of cruelty, delivered humans into the world to find purpose with neither map nor compass, we have done something at least as cruel in making and deploying monuments.

Here is what I mean. The cruelty lies in the nearly sadistic paradox at the base of their challenge. A monument is never itself.

At least, the monument can assert its physical self only when it fails to transmit its idea; in other words, again, only when it is not itself. The monument is inextricably caught between its meaning and its being — the one defying the other — though they are in theory mutually supporting. Its value as an idea-receptacle is not, ultimately, based on any conceptual or linguistic communiqué, but on its fundamentally blunt materializing assertion: the battle was here, the poet lived here, the victims were shot here, the scientist was born here, the boat landed here, the dirigible exploded here, the fugitive hid here, the miracle happened here, the general slept here, the saint was buried here, in this earth, before being moved elsewhere. It is the absurd insistence that meaning adheres in fixed physical spaces and determinate objects that dooms monuments. As if the event and what it has come to mean cannot be ripped free from the patch of ground, like the chemical-laden sheet that is torn off a Polaroid print when the 30 seconds of development are up. The monument is an attempt to place the meaning of something back in the earth of its inception: to insert the idea back into the physical. The problem is, the meaning *never lived there*. And thus, the monument, for all its granite or basalt or bronze, is never itself. In this, the monument is like a photograph.

<u>Introduction, Continued</u>

The 1963 Jacques Demy film, *Bay of Angels*, is a love story of two gamblers who are constantly looking for something to hold on to but always seem to lose it all. The very first moment of the film begins with the opening of a small round aperture in a black screen. In it, we see Jeanne Moreau's face. The vignette-like circle stays put for only a second, before opening up to the full screen. But from the moment that the filmic image begins, the camera has started moving backwards, at high speed, away from the subject framed in that first moment. We immediately see Moreau walking towards us along the promenade in Nice, and she is immediately becoming very far away. The scene continues, behind the film's opening credits, for nearly two minutes, with the camera rushing, in a straight line, away from a subject who very quickly becomes invisible, though she is theoretically present in the fixed space of the shot.

This is the image that comes to mind every time I set about to teach the history of photography: an entire vast narrative and collection of such moments of recognition, investment and the immediate onset of loss. Such a sensation also comes over me in the presence of a monument. And when a monument is pictured in a photograph, the image is doubled. Photographs and monuments are both attempts to stop – or restore – that terrible racing away of meaning from subject, place and time. As with those seemingly doomed lovers in *Bay of Angels*, the union of these two gamblers – photographs and monuments – is bound to double the losses.

Chapter One

It is a commonplace to note that in American art of the 1960s the question of the art *thing* became extraordinarily important. One can trace – to be, for a moment, wildly reductive – two seemingly polar responses to this query. One was to remove the object entirely, into something temporal or linguistic or imaginary. The other was to make it so squarely and massively material as to be too much, too big, too expansive a thing to be the discrete (or discreet) artwork. These two impulses were, in an essential sense, similar; at some point, they became attempts to establish a poetics of that most human dilemma: the difficulty of trying to be *something*. I would also note that so many of these artists were not photographers at all in the sense that photographers understood themselves in the 1960s. They resorted to the photograph, often almost casually – to record or to avoid or to make light – because it made a delightful trail between the non-thing and the ur-thing. It was able to be both at once, or neither.

In the fall of 1967, Robert Smithson took a trip to Passaic, New Jersey, and wrote about its monuments, or rather, his process of discovering and photographing monuments with 12 exposure rolls on his Instamatic camera. Specifically, *The Bridge Monument, The Monument with Pontoons, The Great Pipe Monument, The Fountain Monument (Bird's-Eye View)* and *The Fountain Monument (Side View),* and *The Sand-Box Monument (also called The Desert).* The pathos and glory of these objects, or rather, the glory of his recognizing these objects, entails the following dilemmas:

Nearby, on the river bank, was an artificial crater that contained a pale limpid pond of water, and from the side of the crater protruded six large pipes that gushed the water of the pond into the river. This constituted a monumental fountain that suggested six horizontal smokestacks that seemed to be

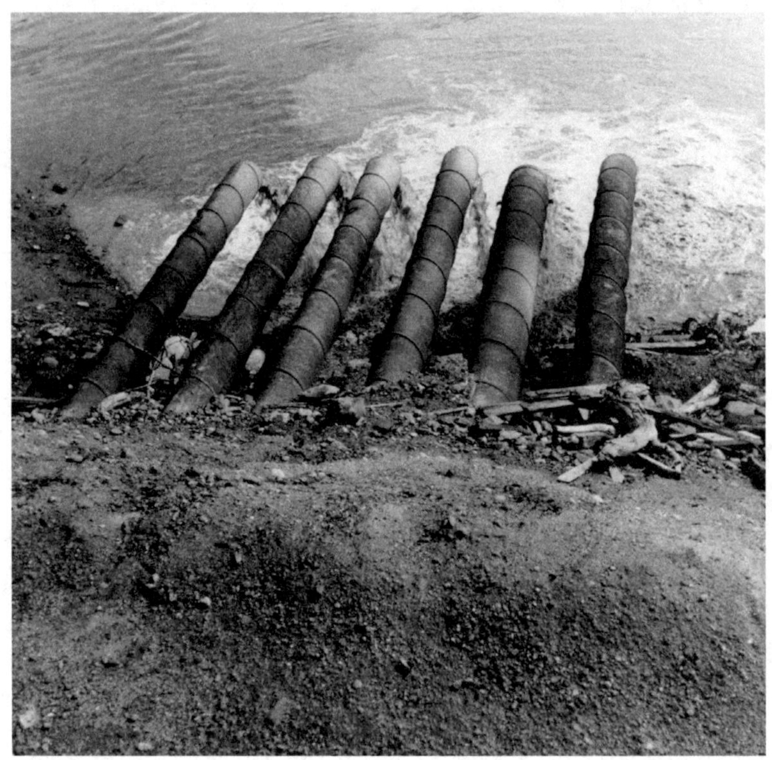

The Fountain Monument: Bird's Eye View

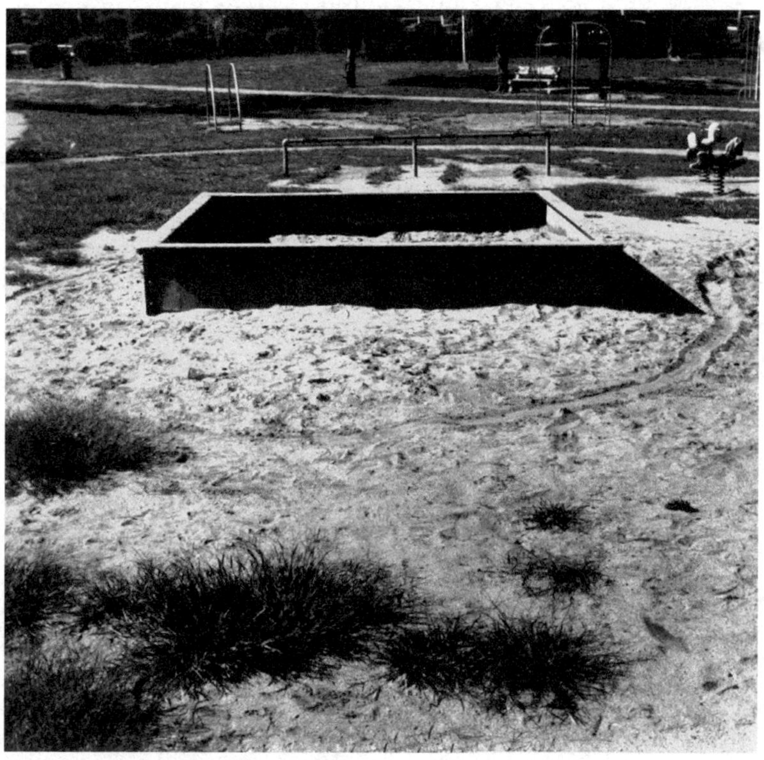

The Sand-Box Monument (also called The Desert)

flooding the river with liquid smoke. The great pipe was in some enigmatic way connected with the infernal fountain. It was as though the pipe was secretly sodomizing some hidden technological orifice, and causing a monstrous sexual organ (the fountain) to have an orgasm. A psychoanalyst might say that the landscape displayed "homosexual tendencies," but I will not draw such a crass anthropomorphic conclusion. I will merely say, "It was there."

Smithson's consideration collapses back on our desire to make meaning, narrative, emotion from a thing, our incessant longing to make metaphors from objects. It's a desire that he liked to push and then retract. He proffered it with language; he retracted it with photographs. For, as in the little phrase "it was there" that cuts off the geyser-ish flow of the preceding interpretation, his photographs, which prove the existence of the thing, also convince us of the absurdity of the meanings that he suggests.

What he did not directly articulate is the powerful way that the photograph enacts this tug between always meaning something and meaning nothing at all. We have chosen it, elevated it, drawn attention to it. It must therefore become monument. And yet, it's just a thing in a picture, and for him often a self-consciously cheap one at that: "I was completely controlled by the Instamatic (or what the rationalists call a camera)."

These objects become heroes (or rather, antiheroes) of the end of monuments. The photographs invoke their victory over meaning something: their triumph of being themselves. Of course, they do not eliminate this symbologizing desire; they relocate it. Smithson becomes the fellow with the monumental problem. We, too, catch ourselves rooting for the thing to become idea. The conspiracy of text and photograph makes the object not itself — that is, a monument.

For Smithson, thinking of these things as monuments is akin to recognizing a failed utopianism in the inglorious decline of the American structural metaphor (building, industry, capital, progress) into dissolute object. It is a dead metaphor in the literal, not stylistic sense: "Time turns metaphors into things, and stacks them up in cold rooms, or places them in the celestial playgrounds of the suburbs." And to the profound extent that the photograph participates in and reenacts this relationship between objects and time, this observation points to the elegiac in the Instamatic.

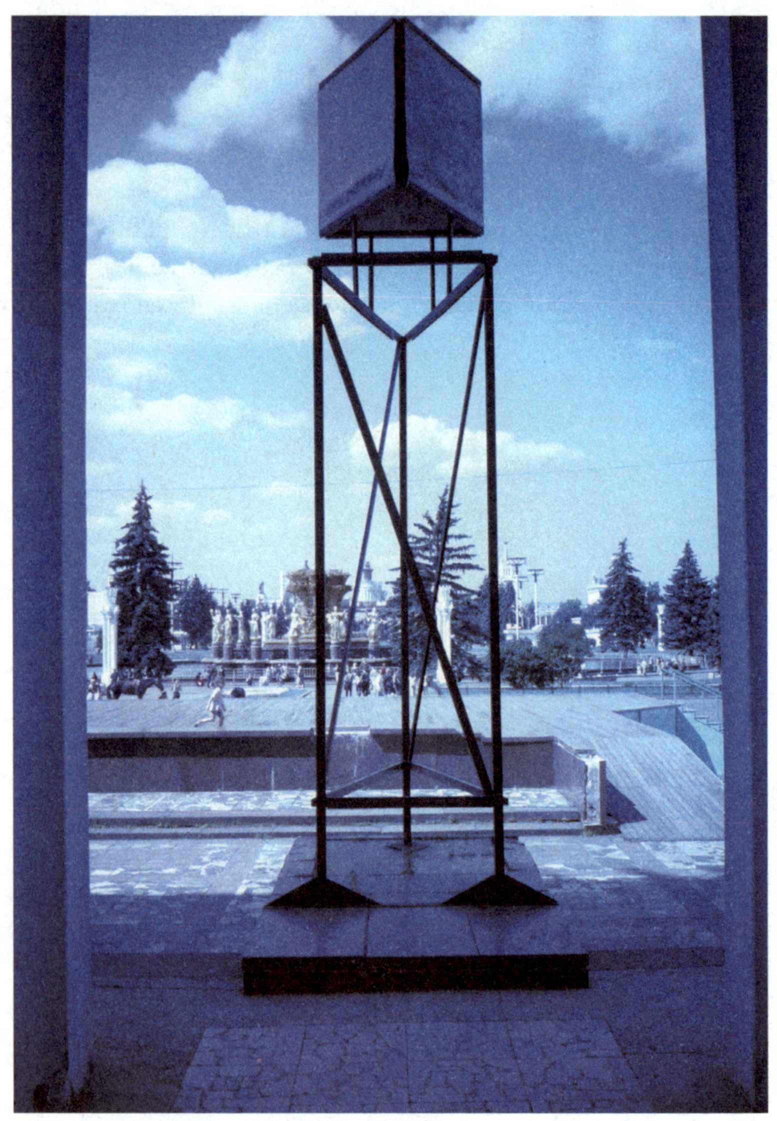

Chapter Two: VDNKh

Imagine a country rebuilt and recodified, almost top to bottom, along the symbolic model of the monument. Not a monument to a past moment, but to a utopian future that is always in-process. Now imagine that the codifying narrative of this metaphorical system disappears. Suddenly.

Illustration: In the summer of 2003, I took a day trip to the end of one of Moscow's Metro lines to visit the vast parks, plazas and buildings of VDNKh, the "Exhibition of National Economic Achievements." Built in stages between the 1930s and the 1970s, VDNKh was a kind of perpetually in-progress Soviet World's Fair, a sprawling grid of ostentatious structures reflecting the style of the period of Soviet architecture in which a given building was constructed, from high-fascist Stalinism to 1970s glass and steel indigenous Modernism. Each structure was given over to displays based on industrial, agricultural or technological themes of economic development and production, including a series of buildings representing the achievements of each Soviet republic. It was kind of what the Venice Biennale would resemble, if each pavilion were dedicated to a display of its nation's grain and factory outputs. It was designed as a place of Sunday leisure for the Soviet people, where they could stroll, eat ice cream, visit a jet plane, climb on a tank, sample regional delicacies (when available), and take comfort in the material success of the latest five-year plan. Or at least, that is how I remembered it from a brief visit there in the Chernobyl-glow summer of 1986.

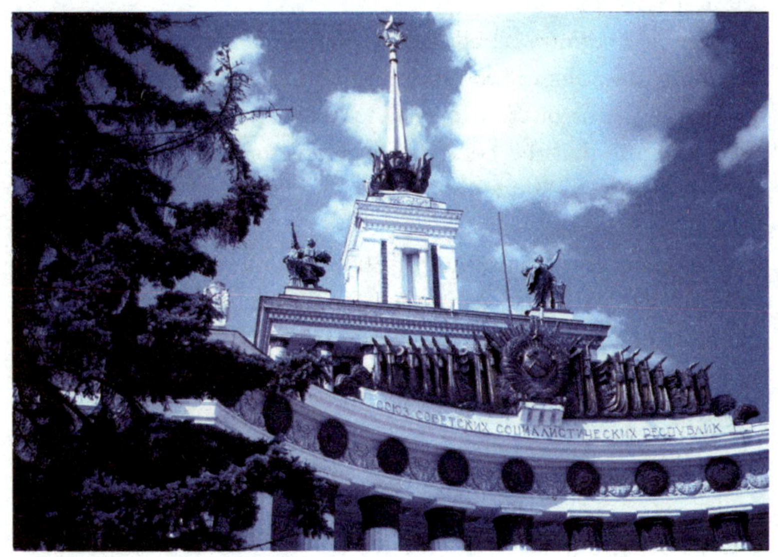

On arrival 26 years later, having fought my way through a dense bazaar of commercial stalls and shops that sprawled from the Metro station nearly to the grand gates of the park, everything looked exactly the same – the buildings, the flower beds, the Aeroflot plane, the *shashlik* stands. Except that now, upon penetrating the unmolested period exterior of any open building, one immediately encountered a dense, dark labyrinth of stalls, shops and vendors, hawking an endlessly repeating array of cheap Chinese electronics, clothes, toys, and pirated CDs and DVDs. And so, of course, I did what any citizen of the new world would do in this situation: I shopped for bargains.

VDNKh is not Smithson's idea of the ruin in reverse, but of the ruin of the past's vision of the future. It is the shell of the idea, occupied, physically, by another and enemy idea. The monument as a Trojan Horse of economic and ideological collapse.

The photographs are absolutely mute on the monumental betrayal that these soaring, wheat-sheaf- and muscled-laborer-clad structures contain. Only in the sparseness of figures in the public space, the blank fields of asphalt and the denuded greenery of the landscaping, is the hollow chill of the suggested ideal that never was, lightly felt.

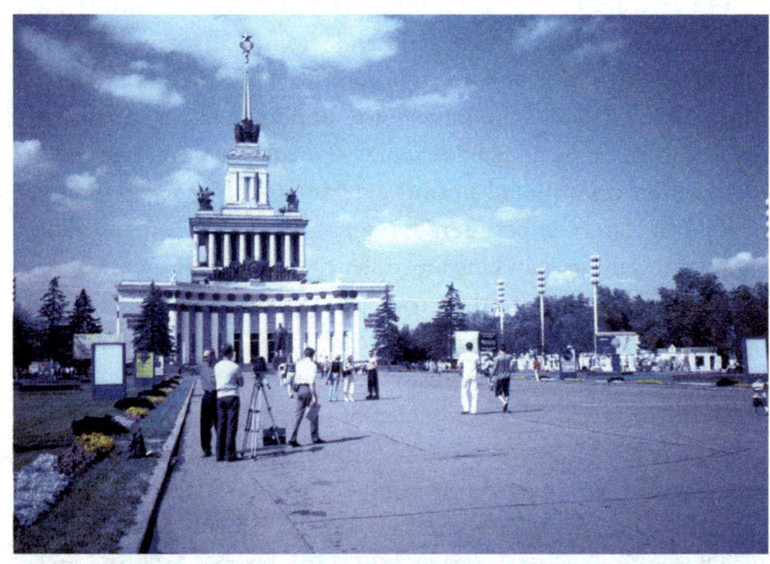

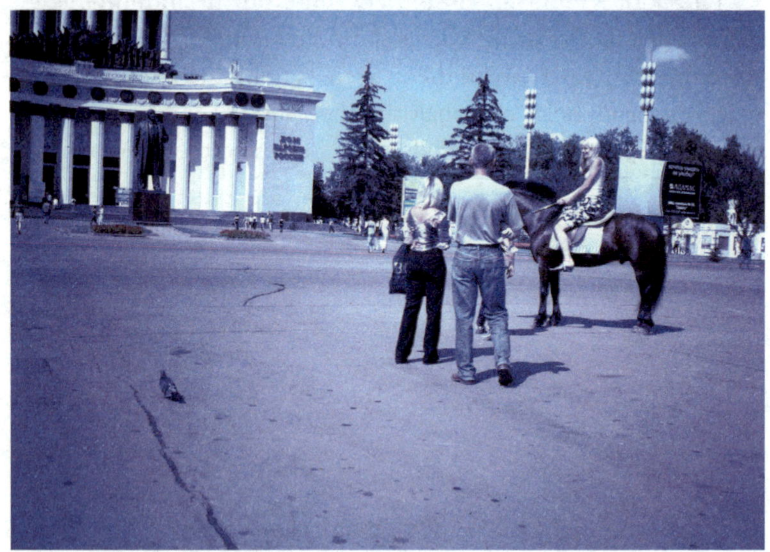

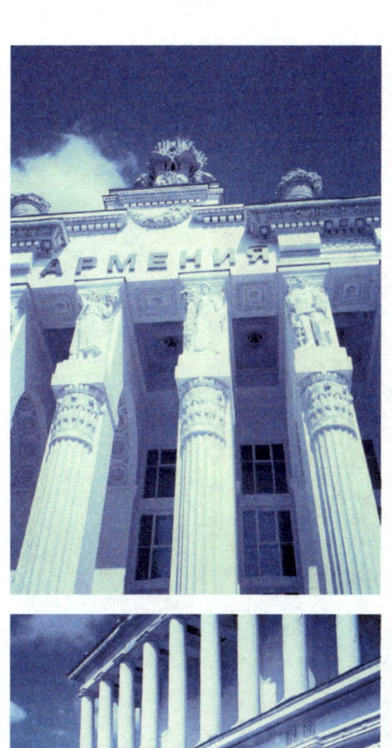
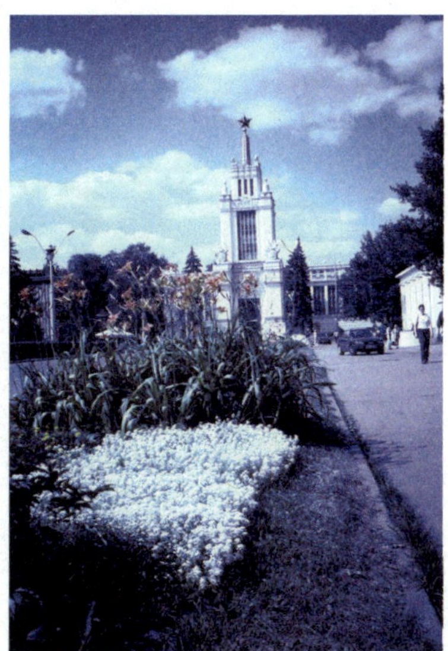
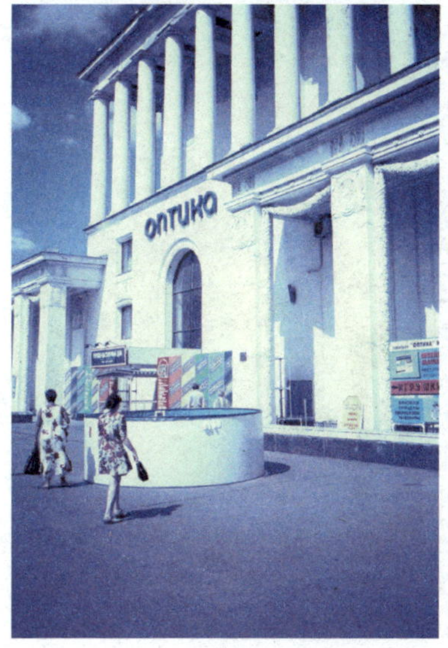
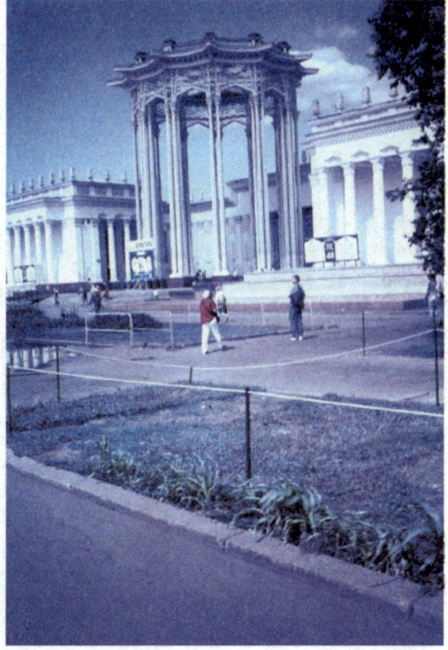

Lacuna Park

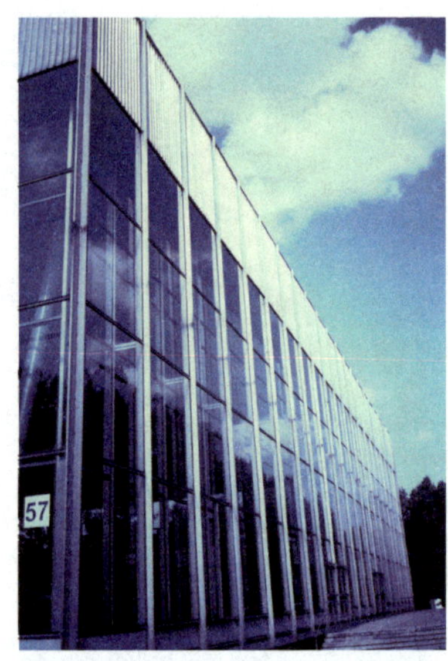

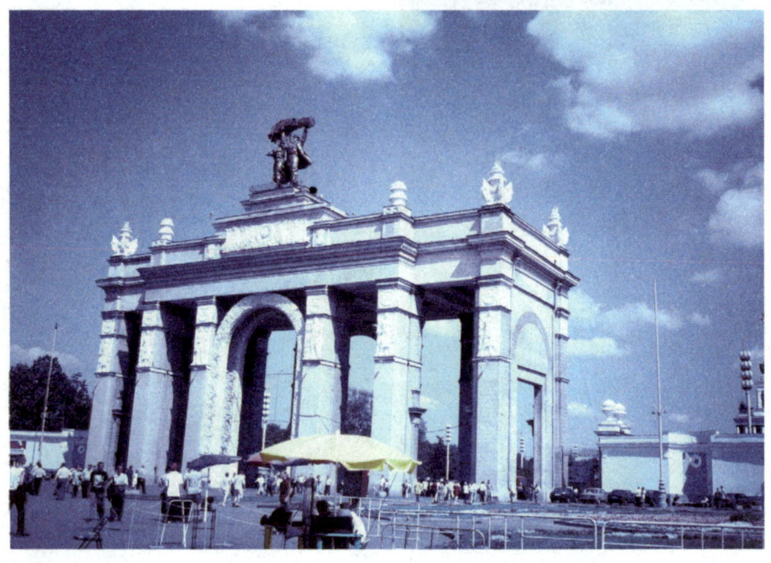

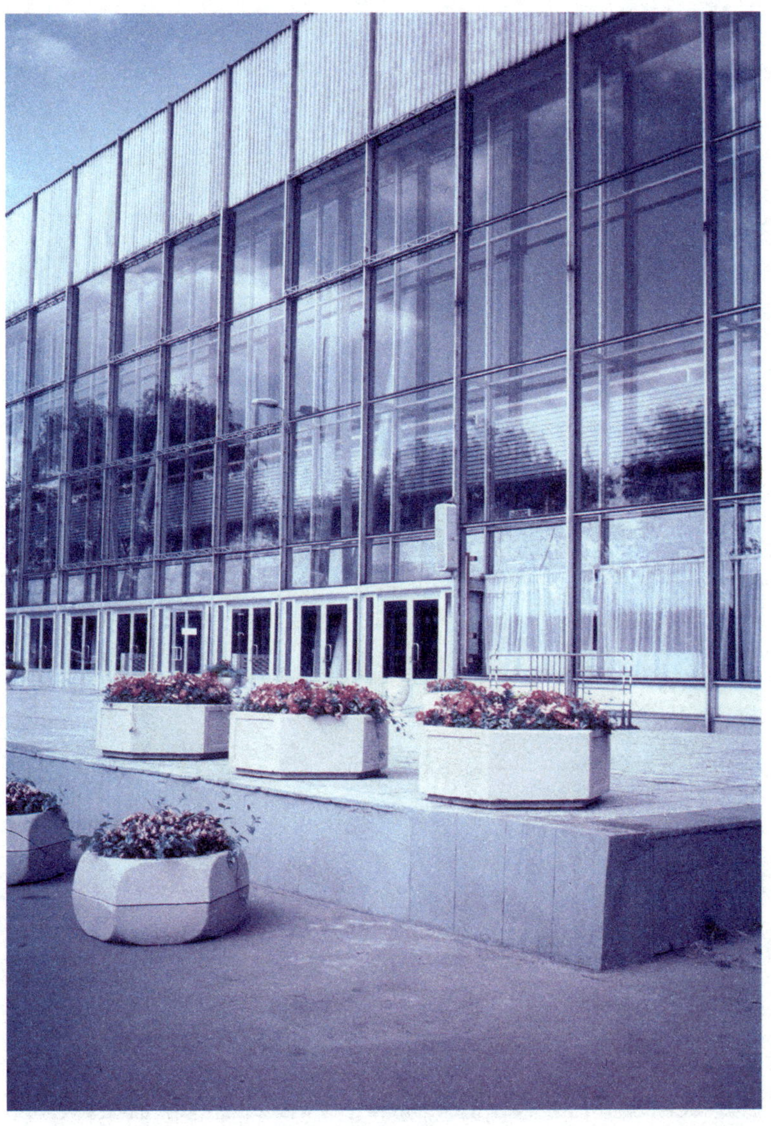

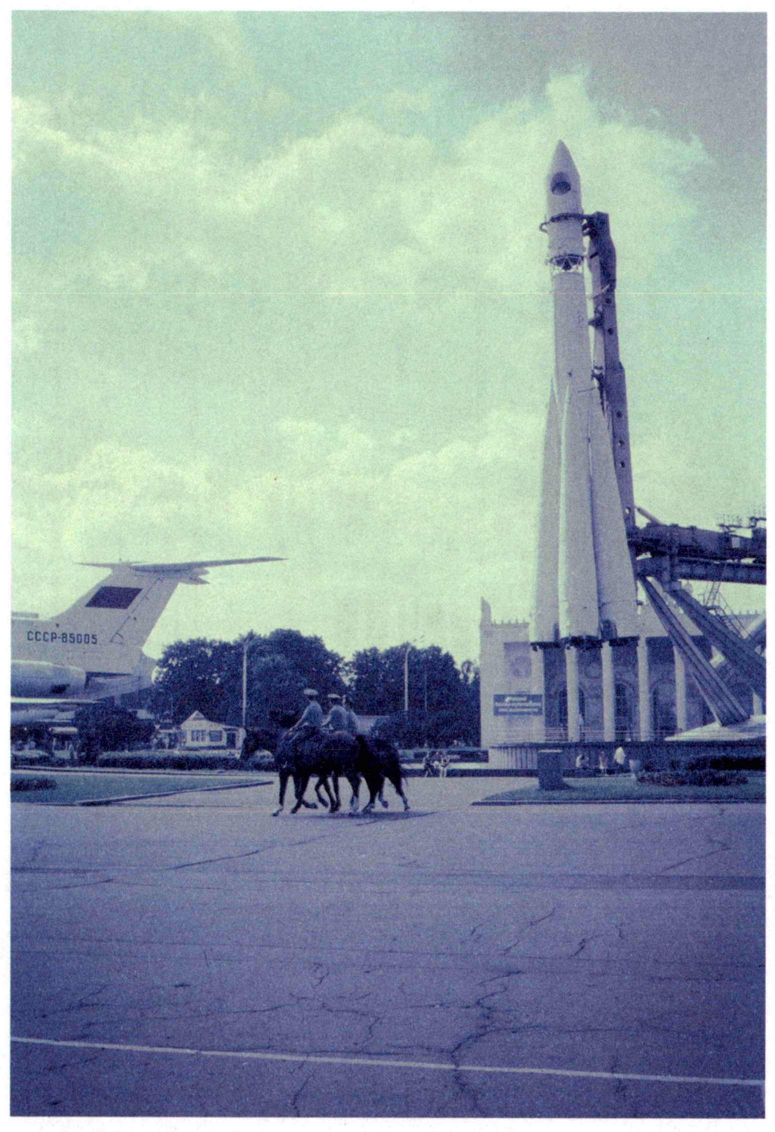
CCCP-85005

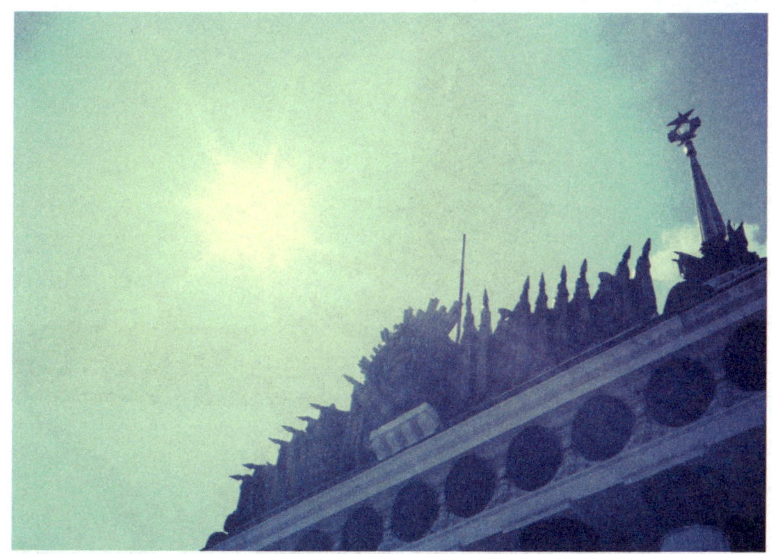

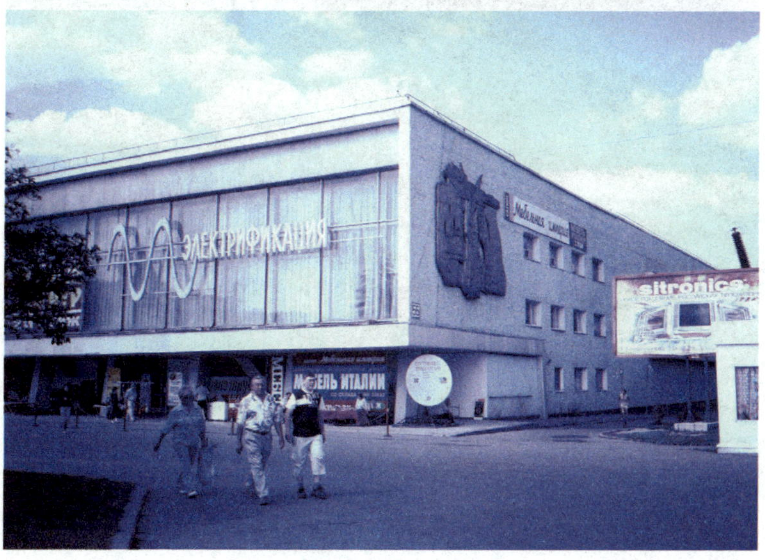

ЭЛЕКТРИФИКАЦИЯ
МЕБЕЛЬ ИТАЛИИ
sitronics

Lacuna Park

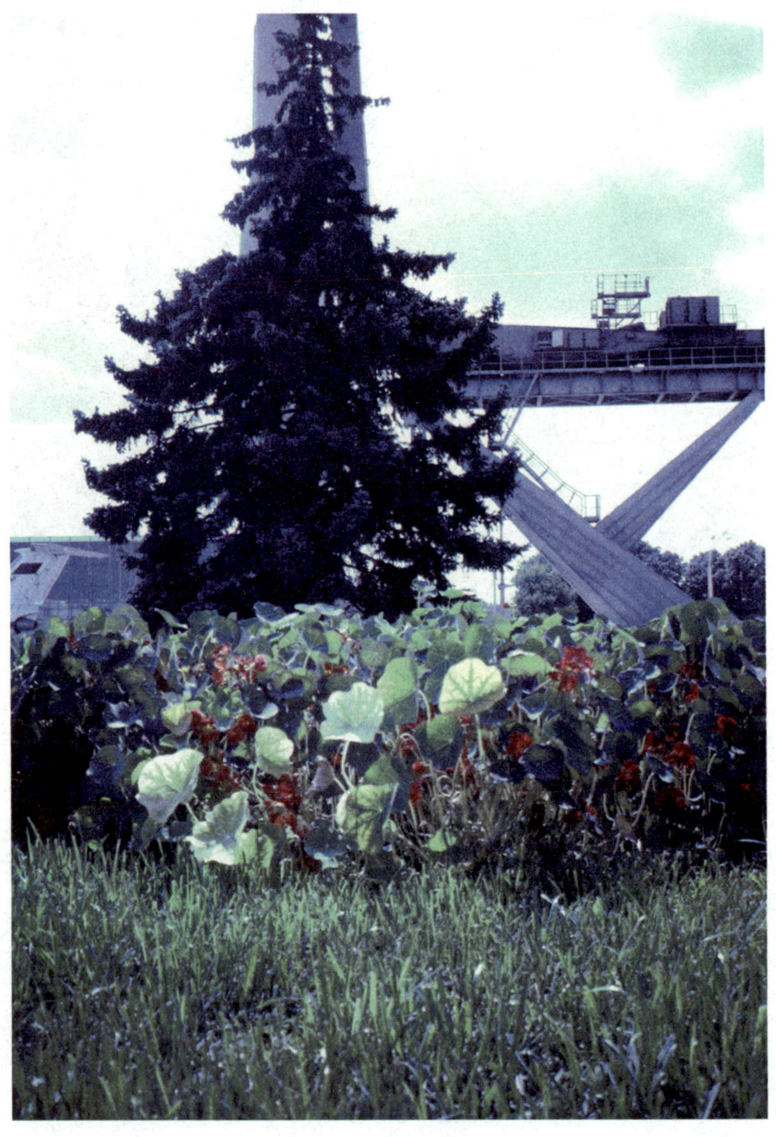

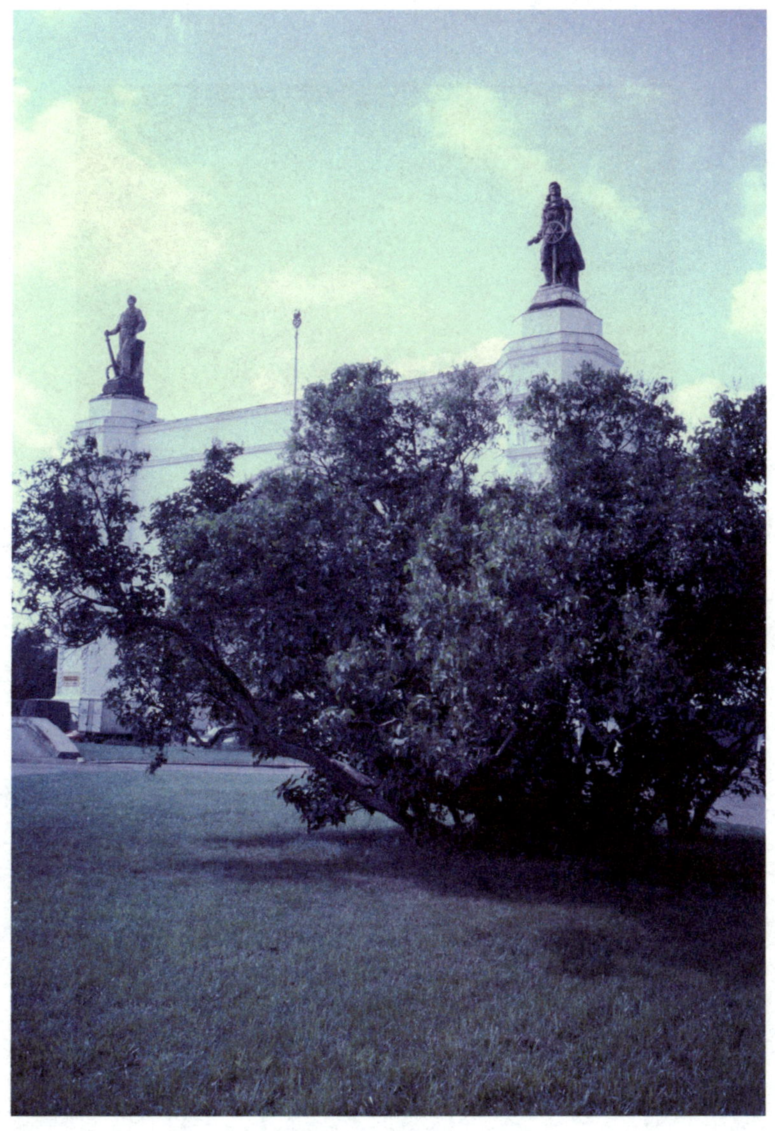

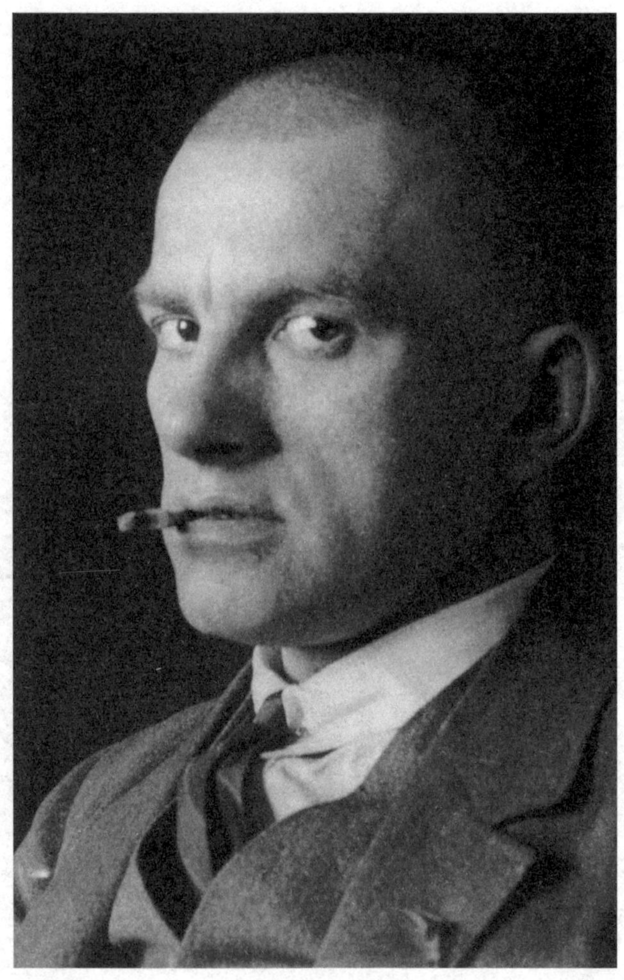

Chapter Three: Mayakovsky-Rodchenko

I want to make sure to say this correctly: this *picture* is the first man I ever really fell for. And I mean that very exactly. I also believe that this hyper-unconsummated romance adheres rather exactly to the dialectics of monument and photograph that I've been talking about. First, I need to talk about the monument in these pictures – for in this case, there was a series of pictures that sealed the deal. The images are all studio portraits of the great Russian-Futurist-Soviet poet Vladimir Mayakovsky. They were made by the great Russian-Constructivist-Soviet photographer Aleksandr Rodchenko in 1924, in the still heady and relatively wide-open early days of Soviet power. Mayakovsky was at the height of his creative, personal and political force – a swaggering figure of genius, veneration, unchecked youthful aggression and idealism, full of grand visions and heroic exhortations. He was the man of this moment. In his plays, verse and public appearances, he made of himself a figure encompassing an entire complex of beliefs and assertions. He talks to the sun; he strides like a giant; he writes poems with titles like: "An Extraordinary Adventure Which Happened to Me, Vladimir Mayakovsky, One Summer in the Country." In this little slice of time, he *was* a monument. And this assertion survives across time, despite the marginalization and eventual suicide that formed the trajectory of his life over the remainder of the decade. All of this information was resonantly present before I encountered the first of Rodchenko's pictures, and they took my breath away. They seem to entail, in their gaze, the most intense challenge to be *read*: the rough physicality of his presence; the ways Rodchenko has described his form and weight; his stone-carved hardness of aspect; the graphic mass of his force in space. The man insisted on being read as both object and idea, and the photographs more than double that demand.

The yearning to understand and touch this man who was both presence and meaning constituted my desire.

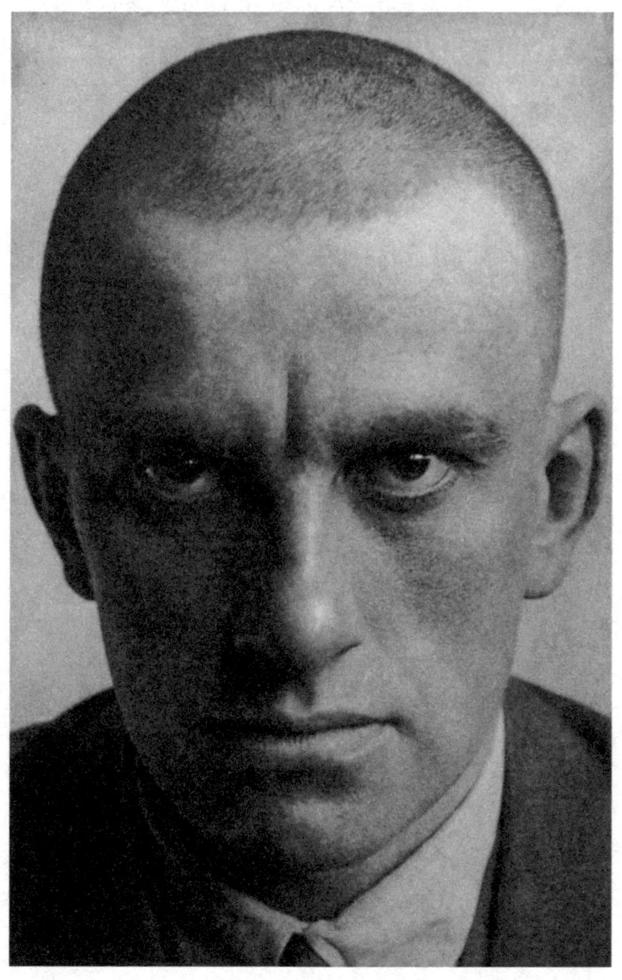

<u>Chapter Four: Two Misadventures with Monuments</u>

So far I have looked at monuments and the melancholy challenges they face. These subjects have all, at least, succeeded to that logic and failures of the genre. But what of those poor things that cannot even attain to the troubled status of the Monument?

<u>Episode I: Dostoevsky's Pen.</u>

One August morning in Moscow in 1992, I dedicated myself to a day of Russian literary pilgrimage. The plan began with a visit to the elegant home and garden of the Tolstoy House Museum, which preserved the period objects and domestic environments that the author lived in over many years during his time in the capital. It provided a vivid sense of his family's high-rustic patrician existence: understated and highly refined.

I then got back on the Metro and traveled to a less elegantly spacious part of the city to visit the Fyodor Dostoevsky Apartment Museum. Located on the ground floor of a pauper's hospital that his father had worked in, it was the apartment in which the author lived for some portion of his childhood. The modest bourgeois flat, neither spacious nor evocatively cramped, seemed to lack any distinguishing traits. This lack of specificity was enhanced by the vagueness of its references to Dostoevsky's life: none of the furniture, objects or their arrangement were original to the apartment or to the author's childhood, thus providing merely a generic introduction to an undistinguished period decor. The only dramatic space in the museum was a surprisingly large, broad, dim and nearly empty corridor with arched windows at one end. Before the windows stood a glass vitrine. Advancing towards the light I perceived an antique fountain pen within, lit by an electric candle. The pen lay atop a sheet bearing a facsimile of the author's signature, and the curatorial tag informed me of what I beheld: "Replica of a pen that Dostoevsky might have used."

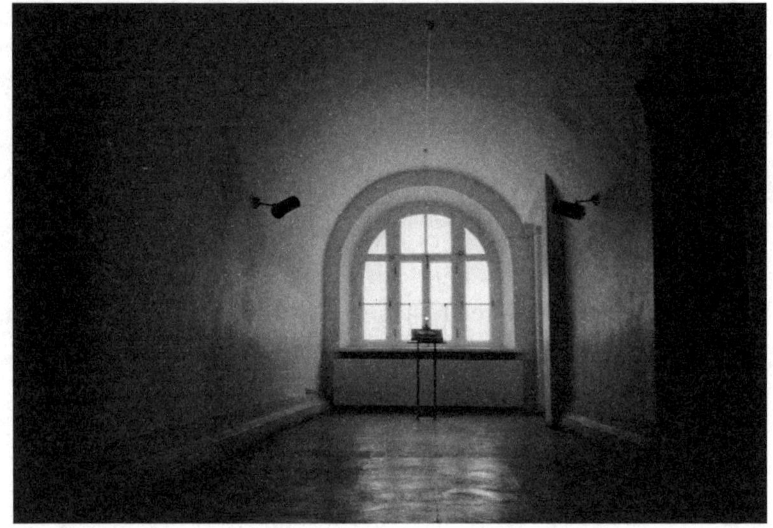

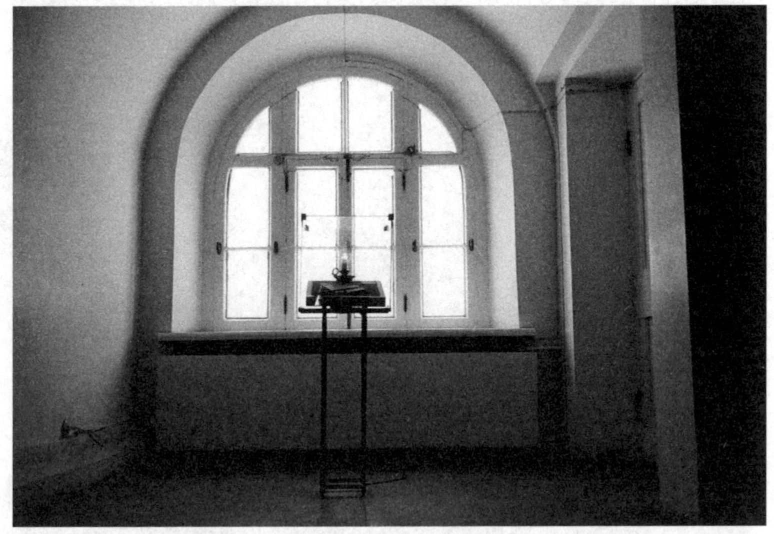

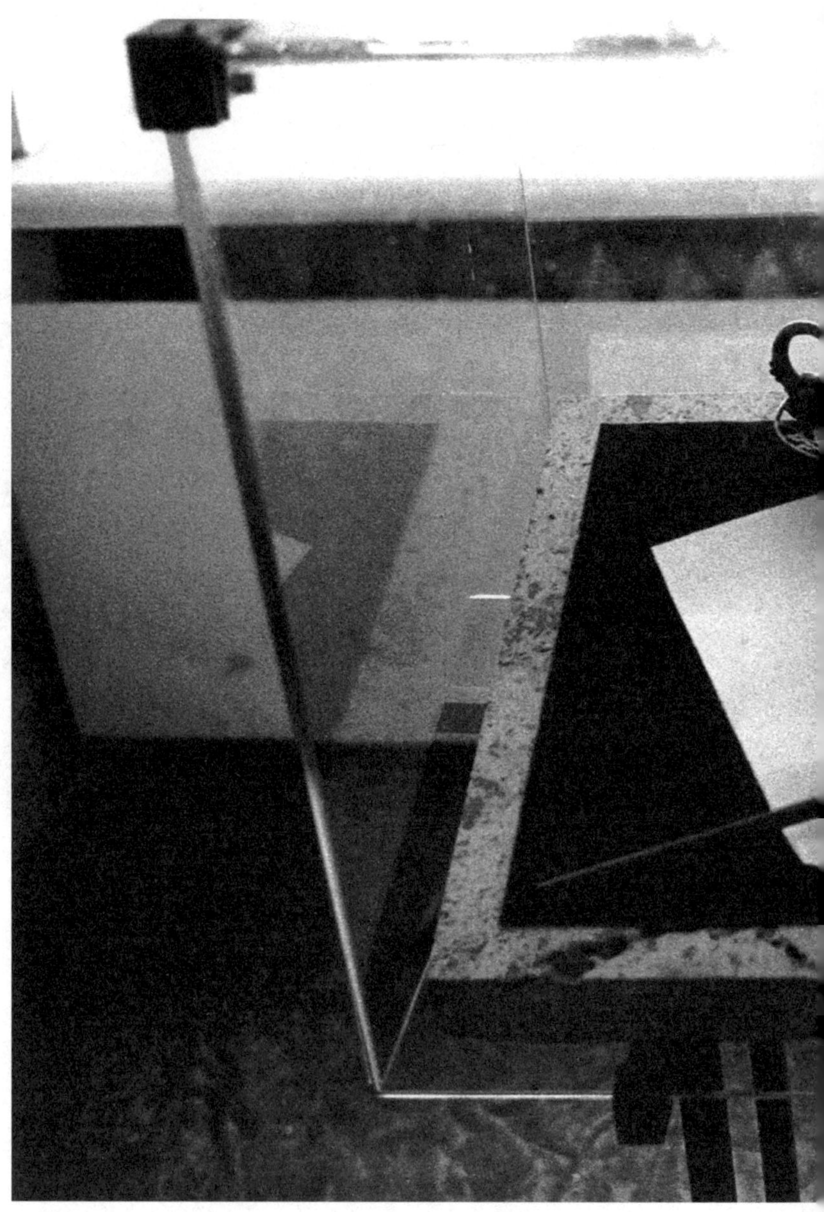

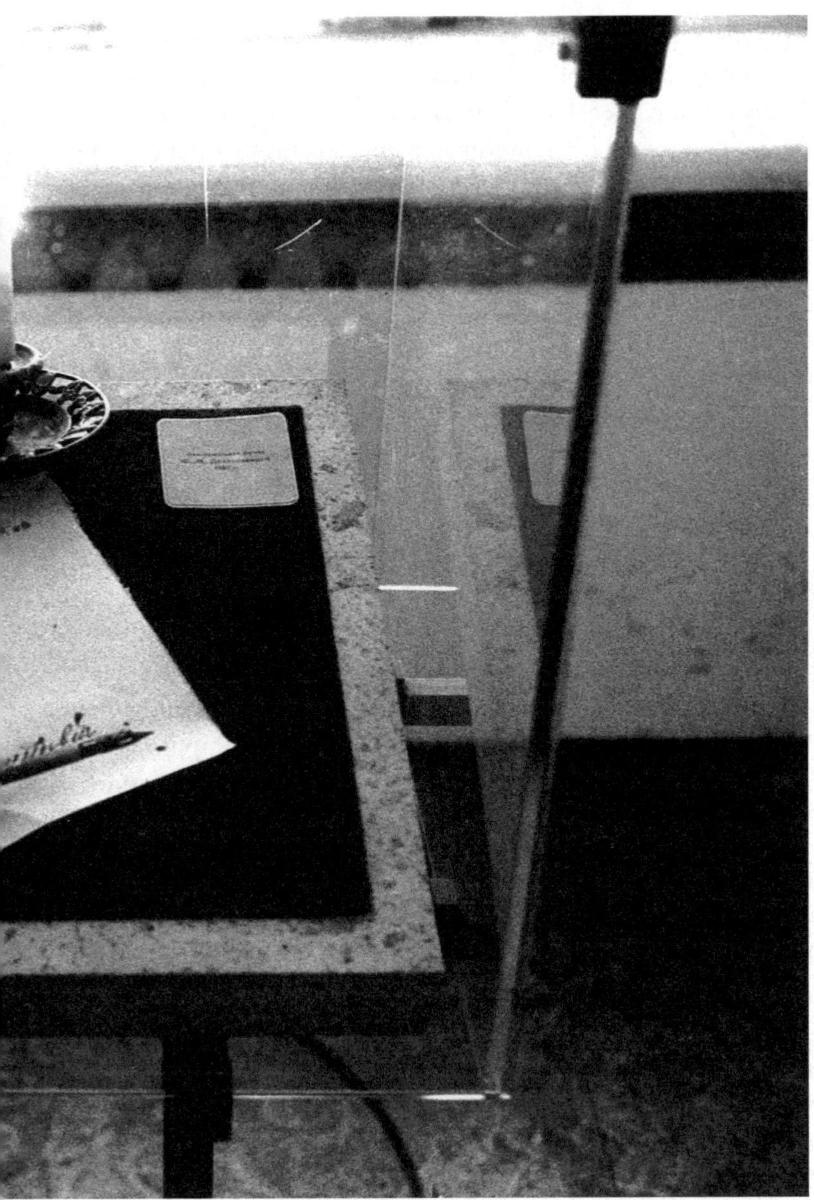

Episode II: Lou Costello

In what seems to be the center of downtown Paterson, New Jersey, there is a small civic square. It is a rather undistinguished spot, bounded by a Laundromat, a deli, a parking lot and some unforthcoming brick structures. There is a modern gazebo; there are some trees. And then there is the central feature: a statue of Paterson's favorite son, the comedian Lou Costello.

The unequivocal failure of this sculpture challenges the fundamental paradox at the heart of the monument's essential proposition. It seems to have played by the rules, for we certainly recognize the heroizing form of biographical tribute, but something is quite forlornly wrong. This is not simply a problem of stature and seriousness. Rather, the trouble flows from the very nature of Lou Costello's meaning, which was indistinguishable from his being. How can one make a monument of a man whose very *mass* constituted the nature of his subjecthood? His corpulence, scale and comedy rejected both the metaphorical and the ideological: his laughter was of the literal, not symbolic order. Idea and presence were, in a very real sense, the same. And this statue, with its unimproved sense of scale and uncannily appropriate choice of a base that at least matches the scale of the man himself, seems elegantly designed to reinforce the refusal of theoretical transcendence that the language of his humor entailed. Costello's meaning insisted that he refuse all abstraction; he was the foolish fat body to skinny Abbott's wise mind. Thus the broken dyad of being and meaning that the monument seeks to mend was in this case broken from the beginning. The very structure of his comic success was the fact that doomed the commemorative project — or guaranteed the unique nature of its humble success.

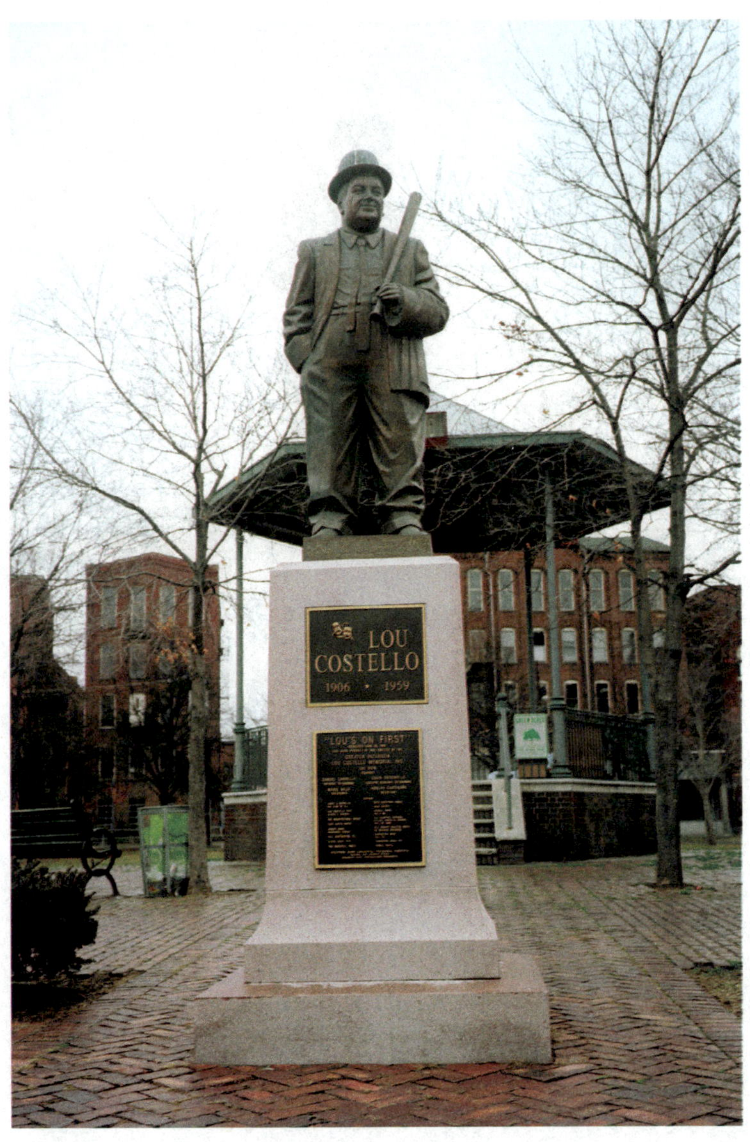

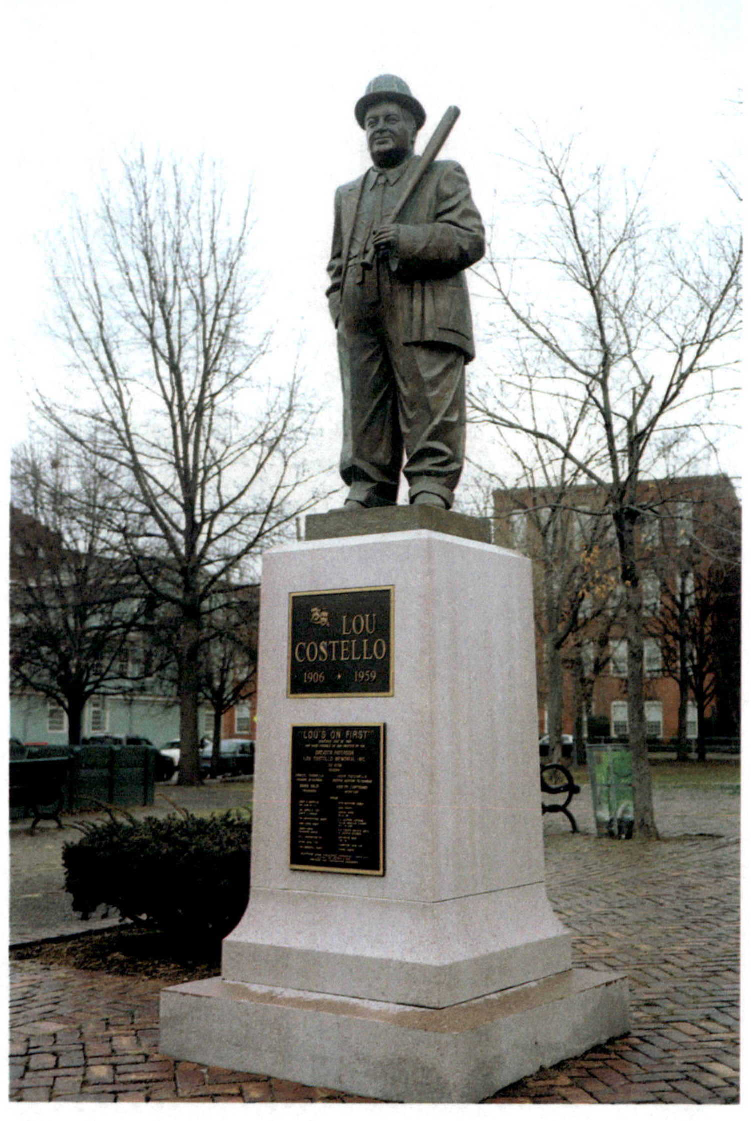
LOU
COSTELLO
1906 • 1959

"LOU'S ON FIRST"

<u>Chapter Five: The Latvian Question</u>
<u>*or* Photography and the Monument as Absence</u>

The following two entries into my burgeoning catalog of failures revolve around the rather contemporary question of absence as an aesthetic form for the monument. In the wake of Maya Lin's violently reductive Vietnam Memorial, the evolving discourses around the experience of trauma, and the ongoing question of representing the Holocaust, the aesthetic power of non-presentation has taken on a kind of popular traction in the monument movement. I am both a sucker for this tactic – who, after all, does not get weak-kneed in front of a void? – and suspicious of what might seem like an evasion, or an easy way out of difficult presentation. And so I embarked on an experimental safari into the topic, with some predictably convoluted results.

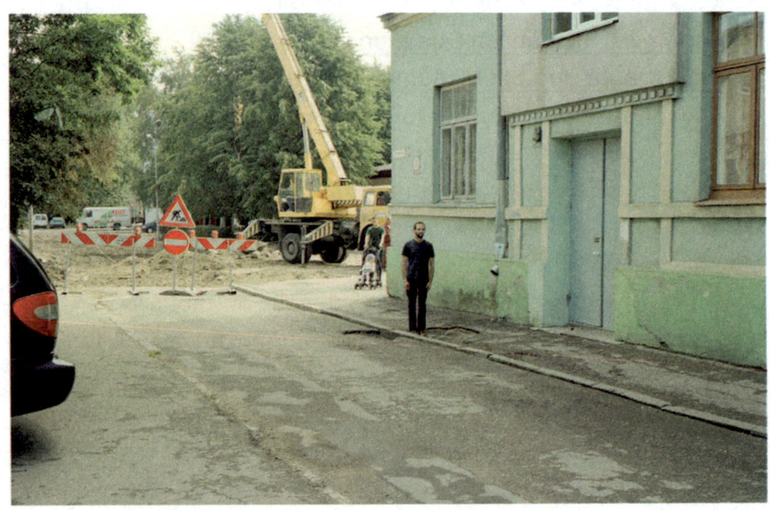

Incident #1

In the summer of 2006, I visited the provincial Baltic city of Liepaja, in the former Soviet Republic of Latvia. I found myself in this sleepy, disarmingly shabby town — a port developed by Peter the Great and maintained as a massive closed naval installation during Russian and Soviet rule — as part of a family pilgrimage to the place where my paternal grandfather and great-aunts had grown up, before emigrating to the US in the early 1920s. Everyone involved — my father, uncle, aunt, brother, sister-in-law, cousins — had their own murky and private reasons for being there; I had mine, too. For months, ever since the day that my brother unearthed our family's Latvian home address from Ellis Island ship manifests, I imagined with a powerful thrill the moment when I would stand, camera in hand, in front of this structure loaded with alleged historical and personal meaning, but which really provided none. I did not know my grandfather, and my aunts had barely addressed their pasts beyond the customs gates of Ellis Island. My father claimed that my grandfather had

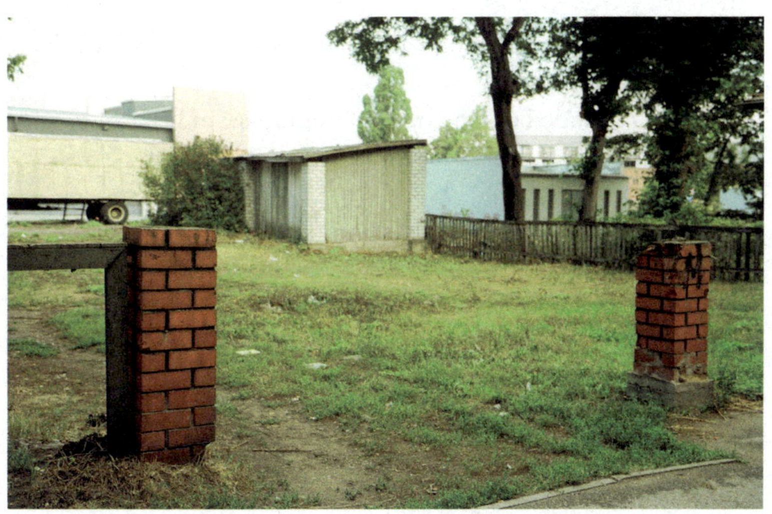

never relayed a single story from his childhood, and my grandmother had never even mentioned his name. The family was not Latvian, but rather part of a community of German-speaking Jews who also spoke Yiddish and Russian. Nothing of that transplanted culture, save for a desecrated and overgrown cemetery, remains. In my fantasy of meeting this dwelling, I would be overwhelmed by the wave of intransigent disinterest that the imagined house at number five Jacob Dubelshtein Street would send washing over us. I would turn this monument-as-absence game on its head, producing a picture of *meaning being absent* rather than an image of absence that symbolized and dramatized historical loss. Somehow, I would produce a documentary action shot of this stunningly failed moment of personal-historical-monumental encounter. That was why I was going to Latvia.

We arrived in the town; we walked to the street. It was only one block long. We walked up and down. There was no number five. I had not counted on this. This was a level of refusal that I had not anticipated.

I was reminded of Chico Marx's summary of his investigative activities in *Duck Soup*. I ask you to keep it in mind:

Monday, we watch Firefly's house. But he no come out. He wasn't home. Tuesday, we go to the ball game. But he fool us. He no show up. Wednesday he go to the ball game. But we fool him. We no show up. Thursday was a doubleheader. Nobody show up. Friday, it rained all day. There was no ball game. So, we stayed home; we listened to it over the radio.

One side of the block was occupied by a pale green, Soviet-looking apartment building. The other side had two older houses – neither bearing the number five – at either end of the block, with a large empty lot between. I determined, with what felt like a flash of poetic intuition, that the empty lot – the only logical placeholder for what could have been number five – was the site of our absent ancestral home. Of course, I thought, the structure had disappeared, along with all the other marks of emotional and historical connection that had drifted out of our grasp. All that remained was a pair of brick fence posts, inviting us into the mute epicenter of our alleged history. I had found my own personal absence-as-monument. It wasn't what I had expected, but it was, in its own way, perfect. I took pictures.

And then there was Gunther. He emerged from one of the two old houses, expressing interest in our search. He quickly set us straight: the large building at number seven had once, in fact, been number five, and though the structure looked too recent, it had originally been the heavily ornamented, parquet-floored apartment building that my great aunt had described to my uncle. Rather than restore it when it became dilapidated, Soviet authorities had simply stripped the structure down to its frame and covered it in cement stucco. The home was there, but it did not even care to be itself. I had set up a dialectical argument about presence and absence that was still invested in the logic of historical connection; and I had lost.

The building had outsmarted me: *he no show up*. Or, rather, *he wasn't home*.

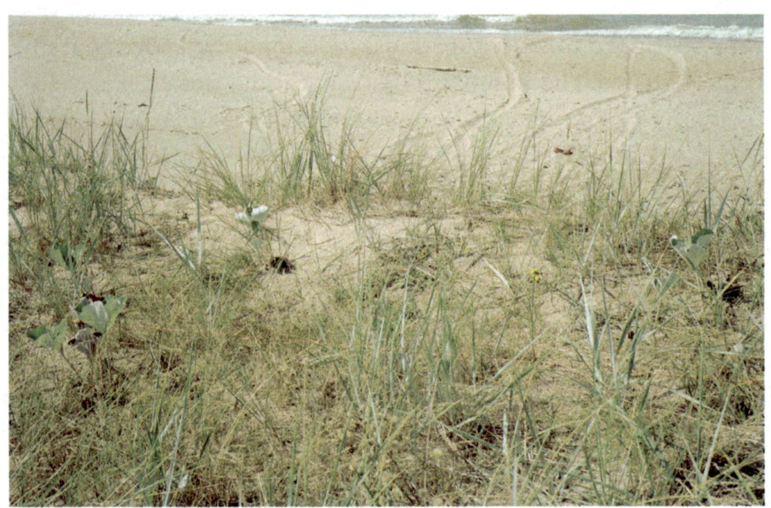

Incident #2: The Beach.

As a kid, I frequently envisioned myself standing – or, rather, crouching – at the Four Corners where those western states meet, one limb touching down in each exotic kingdom. It's a form of imaginary projection that persists in my occasional life as a Sunday theorist. This desire straddles discrete realms in a way that, while still thrilled by their distinctness, inserts me as a transgressor of their borders, insisting on their coextensive geographies and economies of sense. It is, I suppose, an easy way for a little man to feel like a giant. And this often-irresponsible theoretical impulse tends, like the Four Corners, to put one in an uncomfortable position.

I found myself in just such a predicament on a lovely Baltic beach just north of Liepaja. Having found-not-found the ancestral family home, our group's last stop was a stretch of coast, several miles down an unpaved road north of the city. In December 1941, the occupying Nazi forces brought nearly 3,000 of the town's surviving Jews to this spot, and forced them to dig a deep sandy ditch before killing and burying them there.

Jews living abroad had recently funded the construction of a memorial just behind the beach. It was a sprawling arrangement of stone walls culminating in stone pillars engraved with Torah text, laid out in the form of a giant menorah. The gist of the installation was: hope. Given the facts of the place, this sentiment, and the highly illustrative symbolism that carried it, seemed wrong. I was disappointed – angry, even – with this monument. Why would one seek to represent a crime of obliteration, of killing and covering over, with a sprawling, massive object of material description? This was not a monument for what happened here, and I certainly was not going to substantiate the claim by taking its picture. I walked past the memorial, on to the beach itself and, to borrow a phrase from those idealistic photographers of an earlier generation, I made a picture.

And then I thought about Kant's "Analytic of the Sublime," with its recourse to the Jewish proscription on graven images. I thought about Jewish-American painters in mid-century New York, writing about Kant and painting abstractions. I loosely traced a trajectory forward through minimalism to the epic, barren emotions of land art and the austere textual conceptualisms of the 1960s and 1970s. And I thought about the wake of the Holocaust: the dawning of knowledge and the difficulty of understanding in the generation that followed the war's end. I wondered about the evolution of the absence-monument in the light of all this, and about my immediate disgust with the dogged, hopeful presence of the memorial at hand. There seemed no way to defensibly and clearly connect these things. And so, finally, I found myself exactly as my young mind had seen me at the meeting of the Four States: sprawled awkwardly in various directions, and able to make only one true claim: "Look, look, they're touching!"

But we did not linger long on the beach near Liepaja, thanks to a construction of another kind. Several hundred yards south along the shore, beyond a tall chain-link fence, sat a massive Soviet-built sewage plant. It pumped away blithely in the near distance, and its terrible smell blanketed the site of the massacre and the memorial. The perfectly ordinary, perfectly lovely beach was soaked in the unbearable stench of human waste. The monument was there after all: synthetic, rotten, and impossible to behold.

Chapter Six: Volga (The Last Wave)

The Volga is a Soviet sedan originally favored by party apparatchiks and taxicabs. It is heavy with cast steel and appears loosely copied from various Western luxury sedans. I have always loved them – or, at least, a certain late-Soviet vintage that is no longer made – and feared for their disappearance in the sweep of global consumerism glutting contemporary Russia. I arrived in Moscow after a 10-year hiatus, determined to hunt down and photograph this disappearing icon of a nearly distant age. The problem was, they weren't disappearing. Now, you might think that their persistence would prove a boon to my project, a proof that I wasn't too late. But the difficulty was this: they wouldn't sit still for the picture. As a Muscovite friend explained, Volga drivers are known to be the city's worst and the most relentless. Confident that the deadly mass of their vehicles will crush all others, they careen around heedlessly, stopping for nobody and hurtling at high speed. Far from being forgotten, the older vehicles are still coveted.

I did my best, despite the ludicrous handicap of a point-and-shoot camera with a shutter delay, but I mostly missed. Unless, of course, they were parked. But any sporting person knows that you can't arrest what has already stopped.

And so I failed in the hunt for a monument that was unwilling: that refused to become object rather than actor. Vintage Volgas have so far succeeded in their desperate drive not to become still, or monument. The last wave resists the sculpture, and the photograph reports on this refusal.

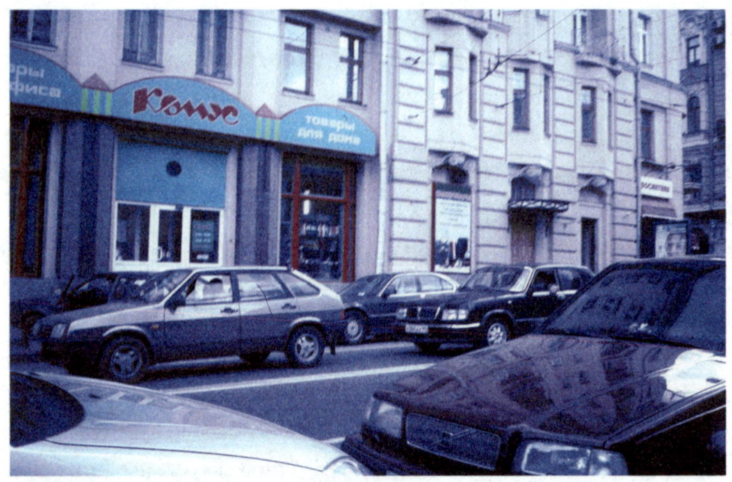
Конус
товары
для дома

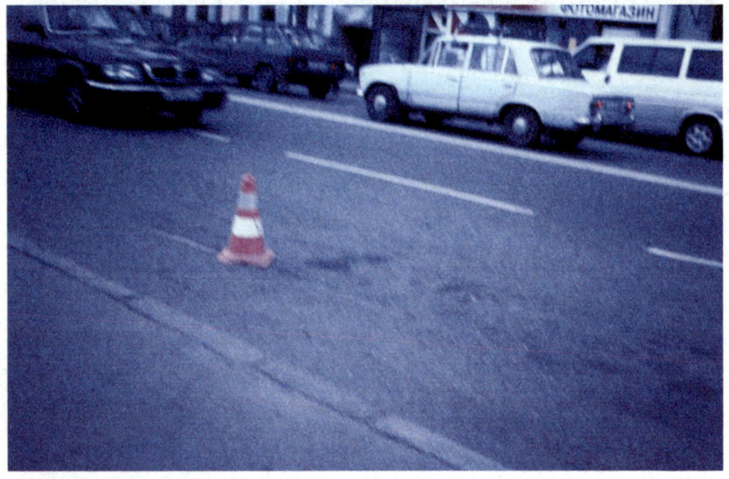
АВТОМАГАЗИН

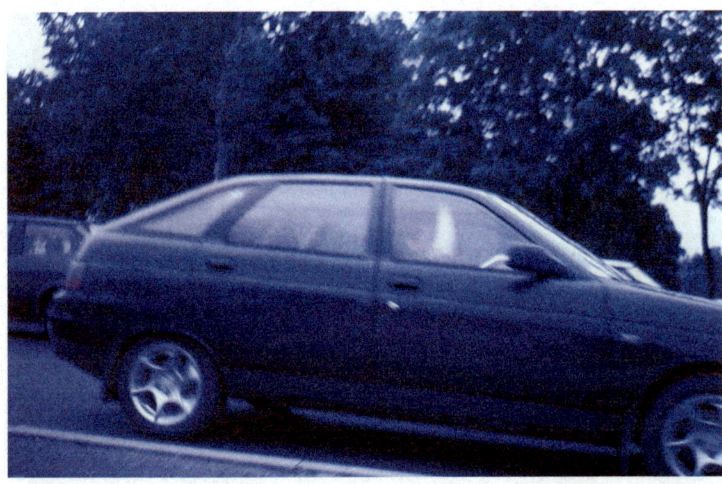

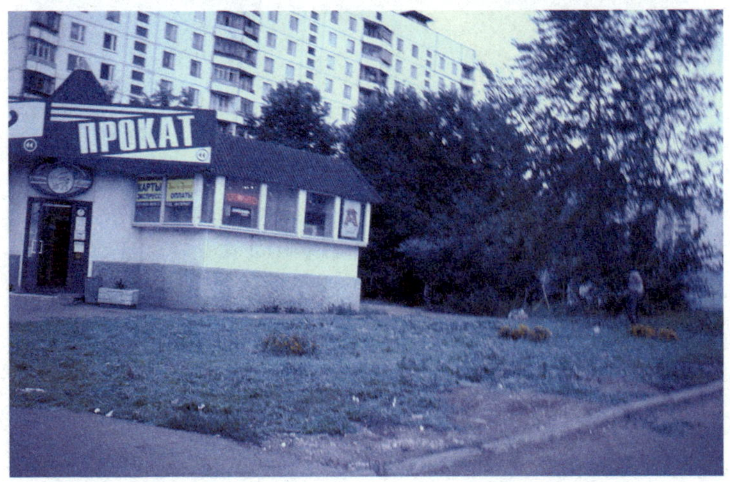
ПРОКАТ
КАРТЫ
ЭКСПРЕСС
ОПЛАТЫ

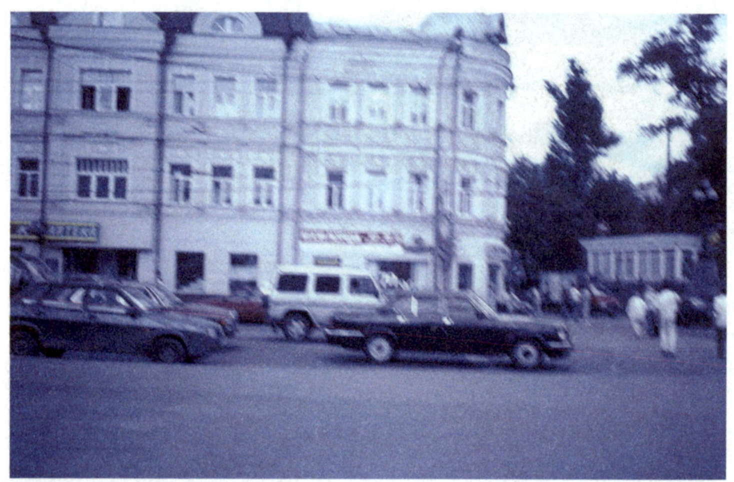

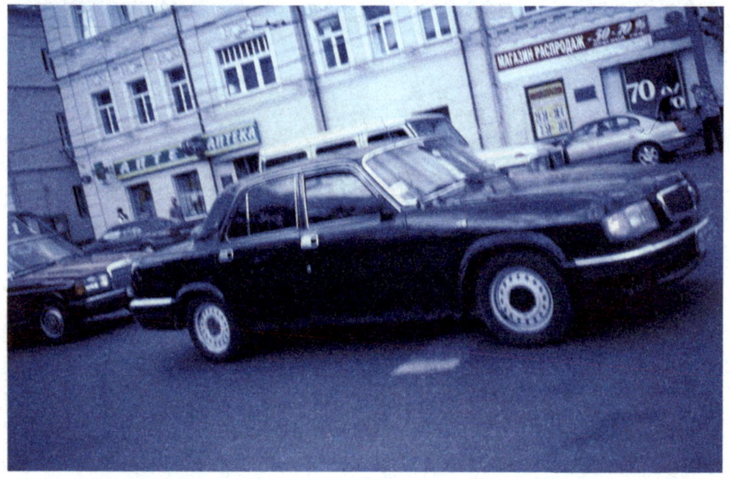

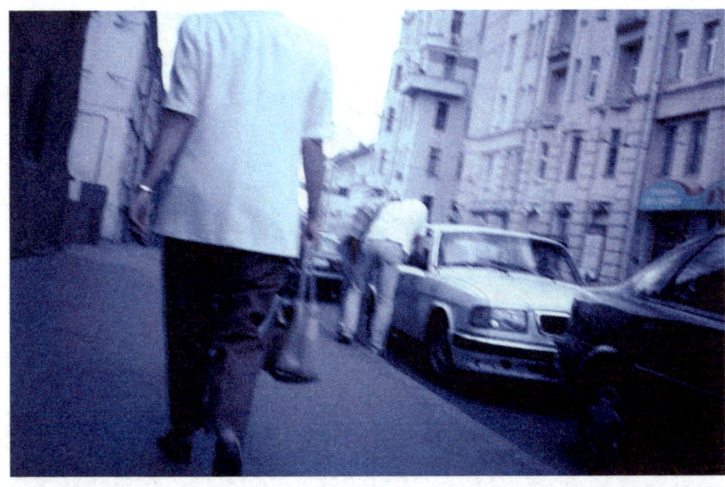

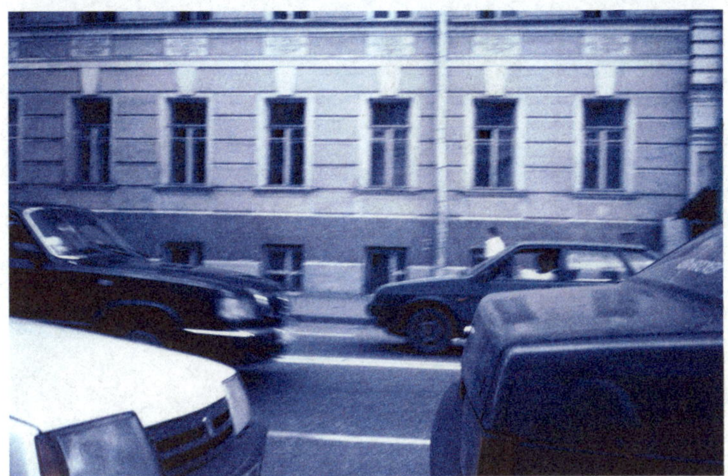

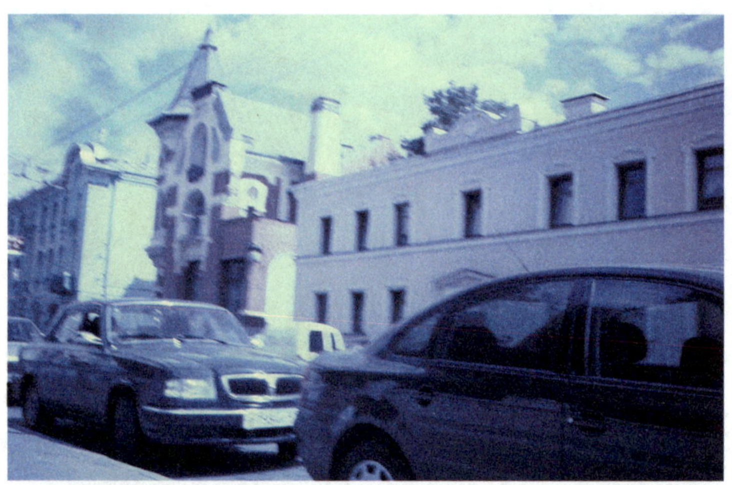

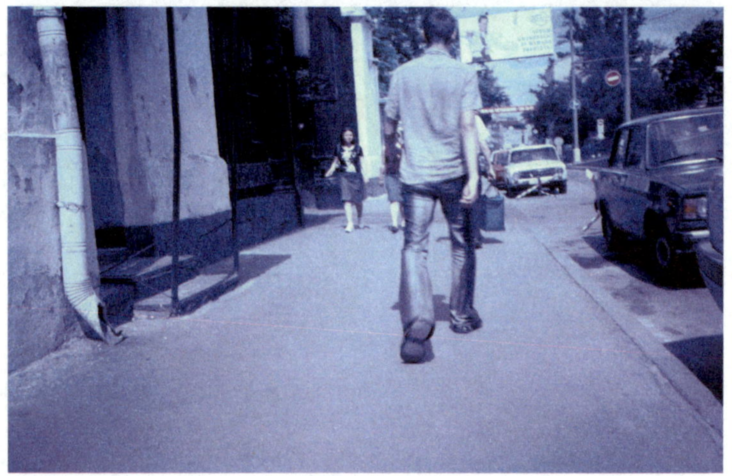

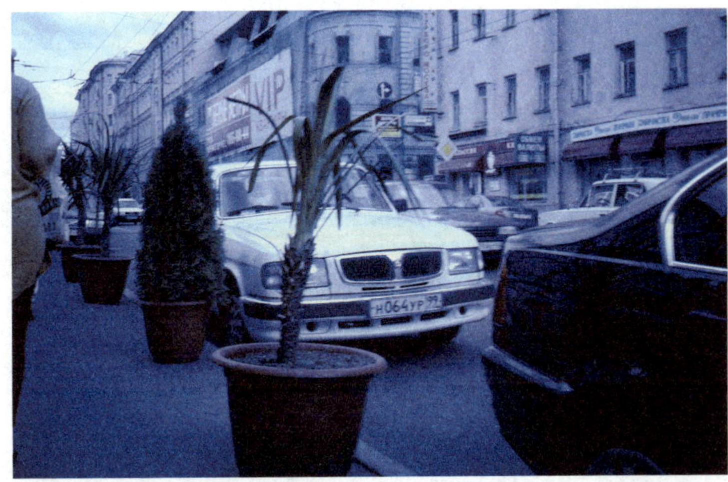

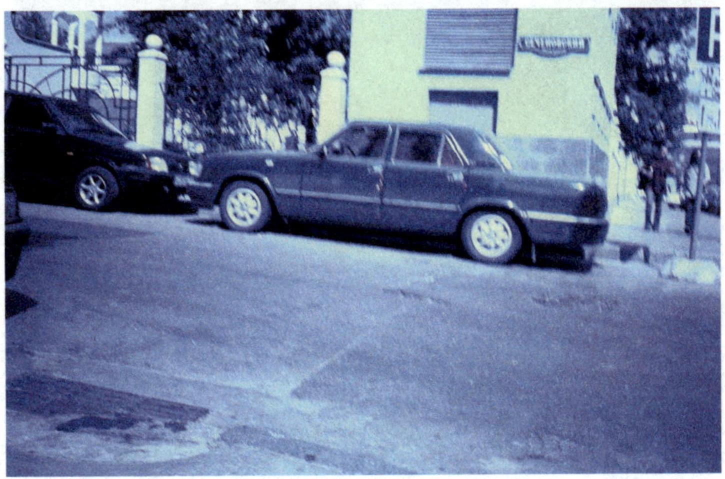

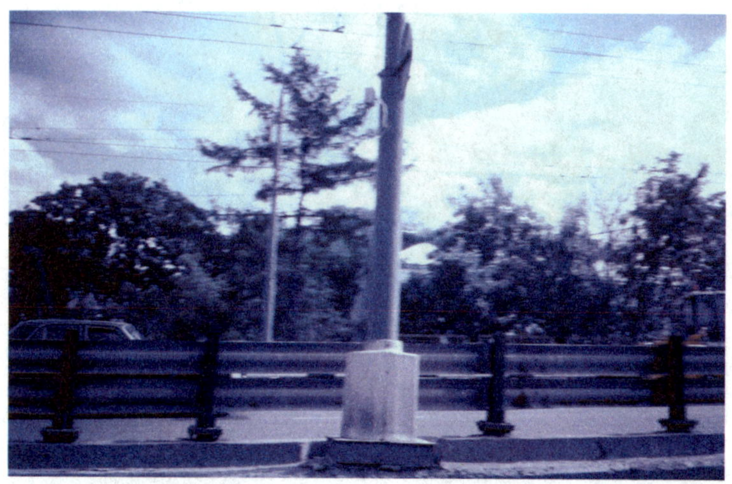

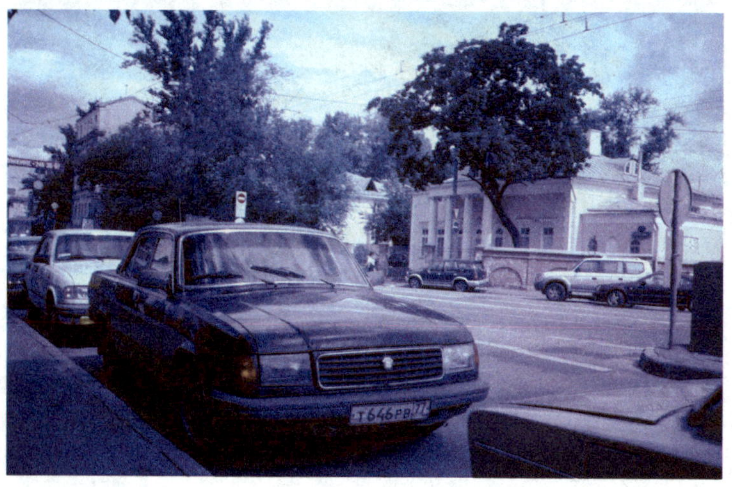

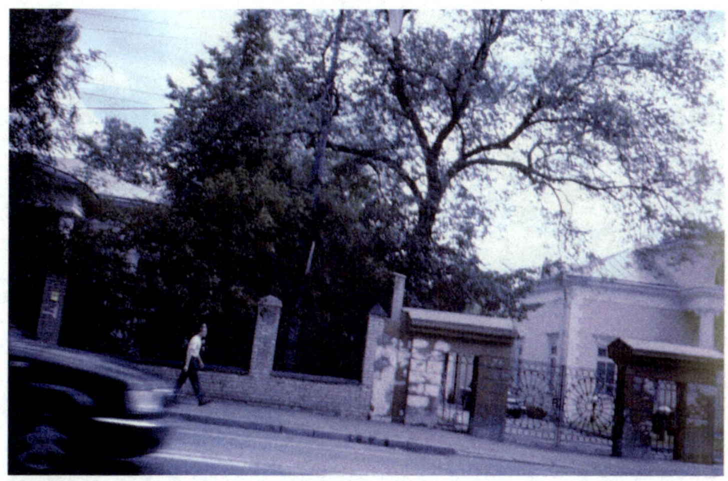

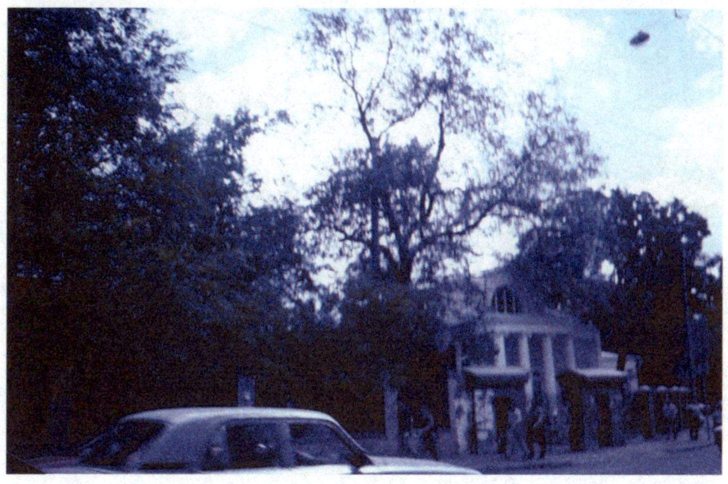

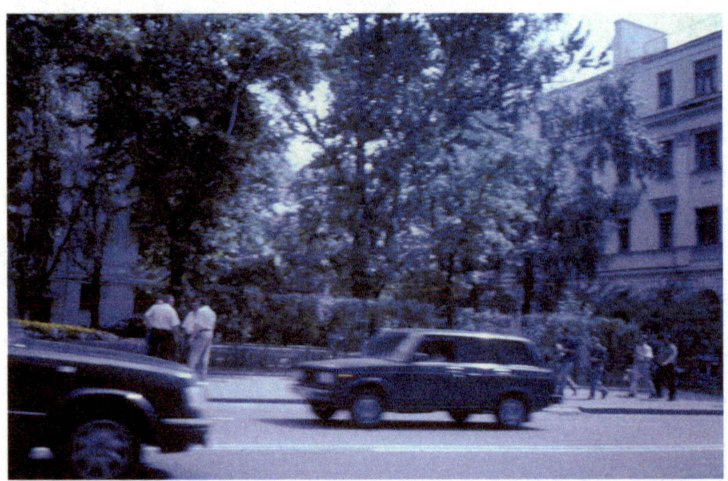

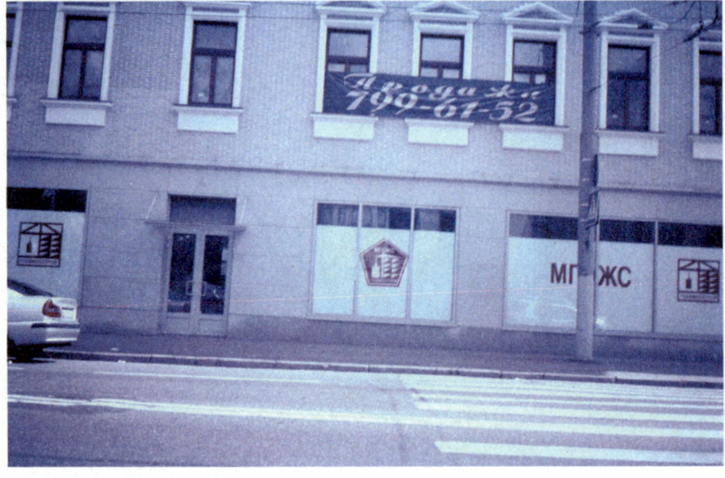

Продажа
799-61-52
МГ ЖС

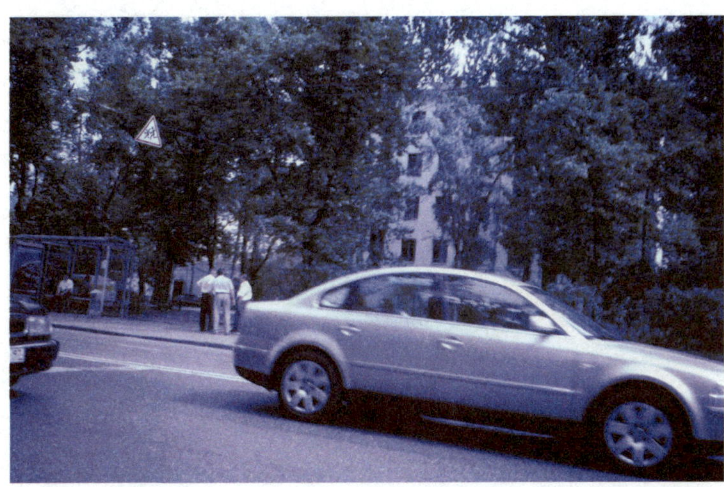

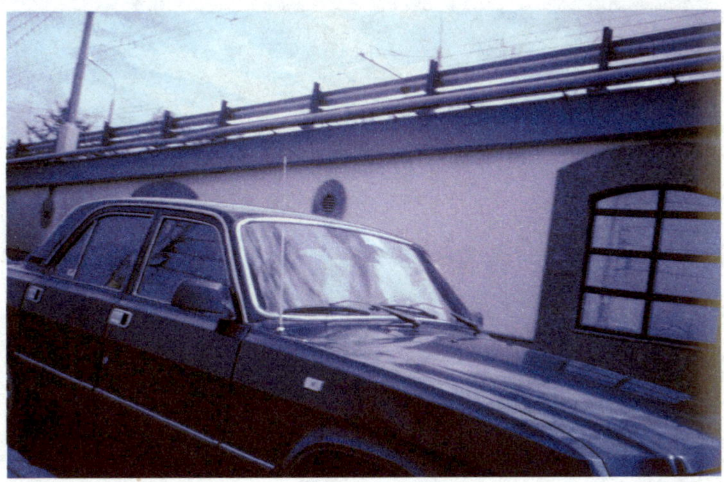

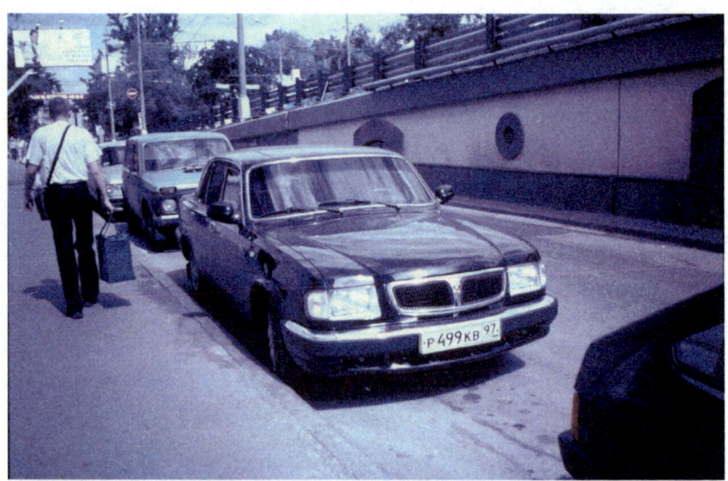

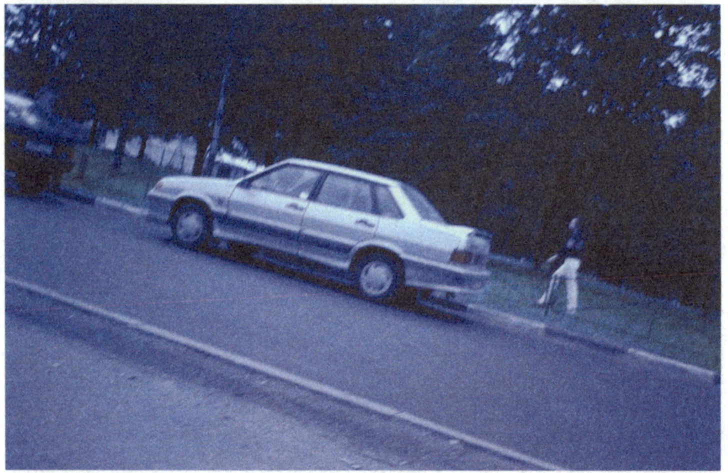

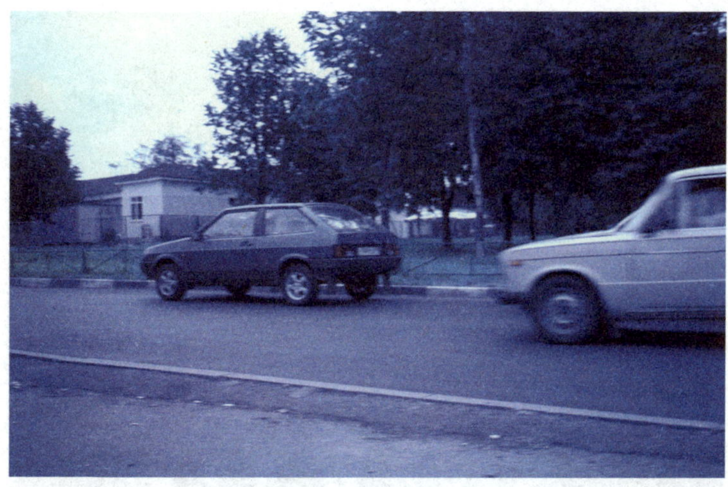

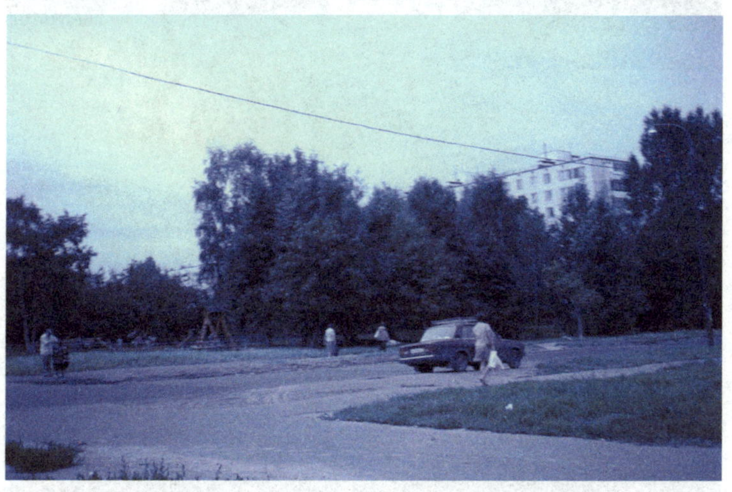

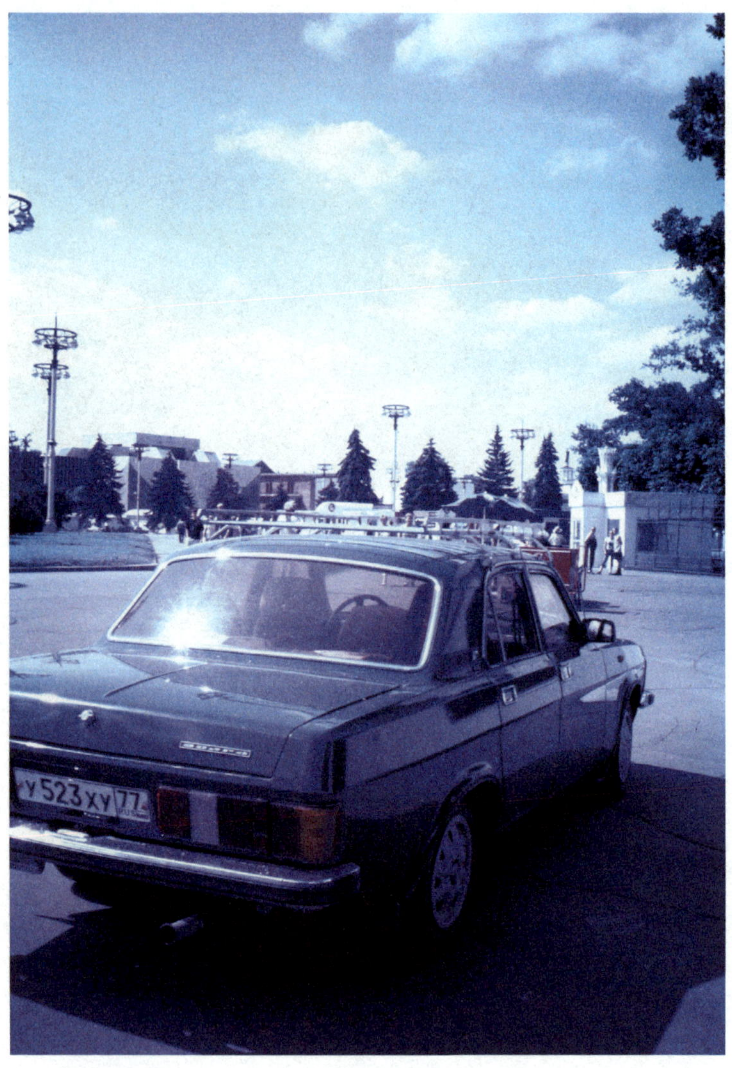

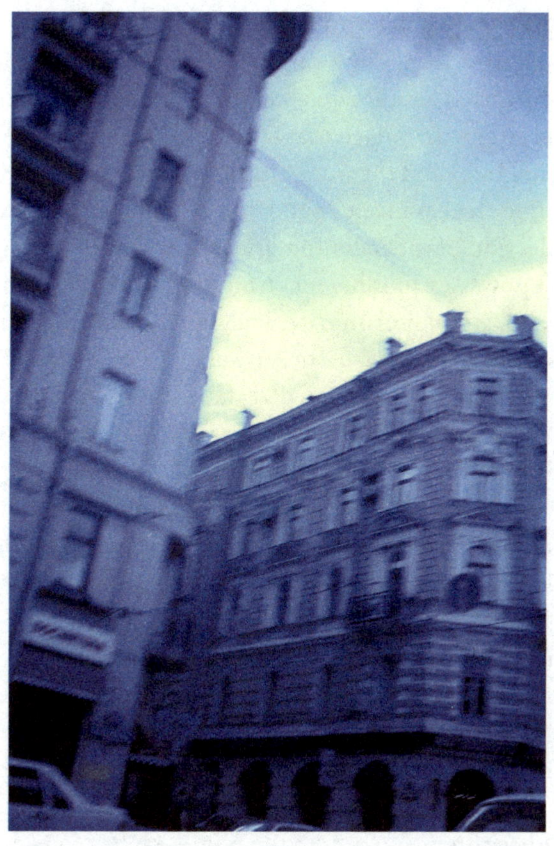

Chapter Seven: From Kracauer to Epstein

In his melancholy 1927 essay on photography, titled cagily, "Photography," Siegfried Kracauer concentrates on the fundamental distinction between the image that is made by memory (what he calls the monogram) and the image made by photography. He argues that memory makes images out of what it values, so that an individual's collection of mental monograms holds on to its powerful worth and possesses an inherent "truth value." Photographs, on the other hand, are indiscriminate. They will make an image of anything, and even when the chosen subject had value and meaning in its moment of recording, that value dissipates progressively over time and across viewers. The photograph fails because it drifts towards indifference; it empties out.

But Kracauer was not saying this while looking at a picture of a monument, and it certainly was not an Ektachrome slide that my Uncle Irv had made of the Alexander Column in front of the Hermitage in Leningrad in 1960.

In the summer of that year, Irv and Sara Epstein, of Aspen Way in Elkins Park, PA, embarked on a tour that took them from London across Nordic capitals (Copenhagen, Helsinki) to Warsaw and Leningrad. That's probably not the exact order, but that's my order, and the itinerary is gleaned from labeled slide boxes.

Obviously, I have an investment in the photographer, in trying to read his experience through the frames that he made. I have a narrative matrix in which to situate these situations: the Russian immigrant kid from the *shtetl* returning as the affluent American; the would-be artist, enamored of early Modernism, but too poor to pursue anything other than building the family dress business. This particular identification allowed me to think of what he wanted himself to mean in front of the monument. But then I realized: That wish is common.

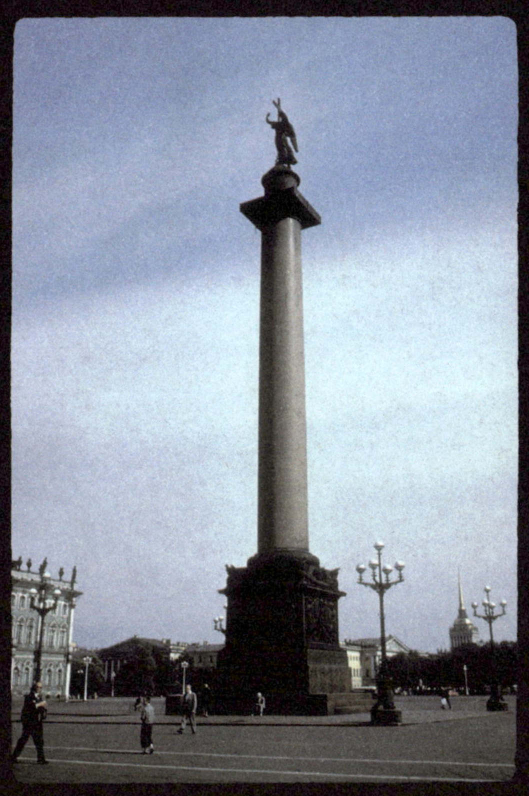

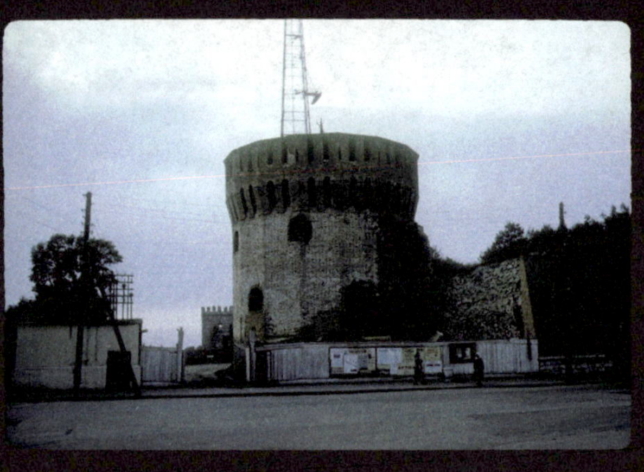

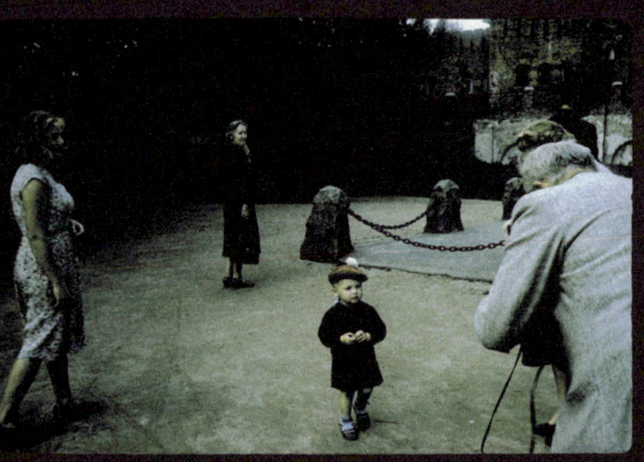

The desire that these images express does not readily reduce to Susan Sontag's famous critique of tourist photography as a guard against idleness, providing a phantom job within the capitalist discourse of the American (or Japanese, or German) work ethic. Nor is it, as she claims, a form of displaced colonialism in the era of disappearing empires. Contrary to Sontag's damning readings, the tourist photograph is not always an extension of a consumer economy's blunt equation of acquisition with success.

The photograph of the monument can also be read as an expression of our desire to mean something when we are away, ripped from the usual props and contexts of home that obfuscate questions of the existential. In front of the monument, we make the psychic effort to bridge the physical and the emotional: to tie a mental movement of ideas and feelings to a fact of presence.

It is this yearning that fills Kracauer's constantly emptying vessel. Suddenly, the lonesome drift of the photograph that he decries has found a category of experience to which its supposed inadequacy is equal. The photograph of the monument can thus be seen to bear an embedded transaction, or aspiration, of meaning. The image inscribes this hope in its frame.

In tourism, that is, in the physical world at large, the declared monument is that which loses, for the most part, the metaphorical value with which it has been specially vested. As with Smithson, the person (the traveler) and their presence, is that which may become monumental. The photograph, including the acts of making, having and showing it, reasserts and reformulates for the individual the core paradox of the monument: *you* being *here* makes meaning.

Lacuna Park

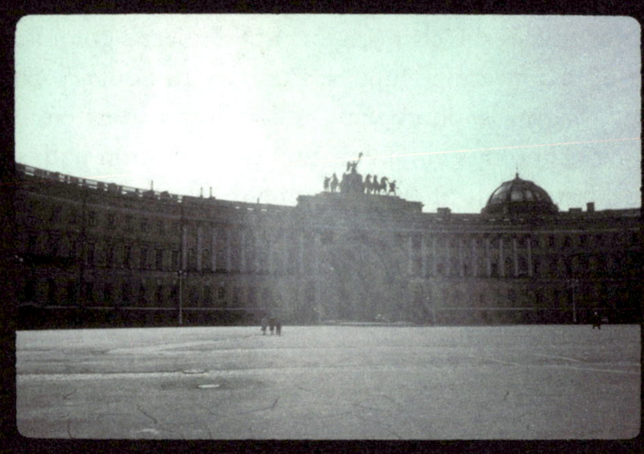

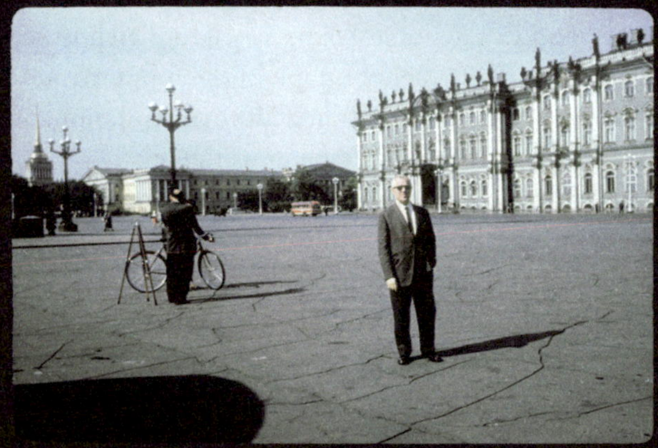

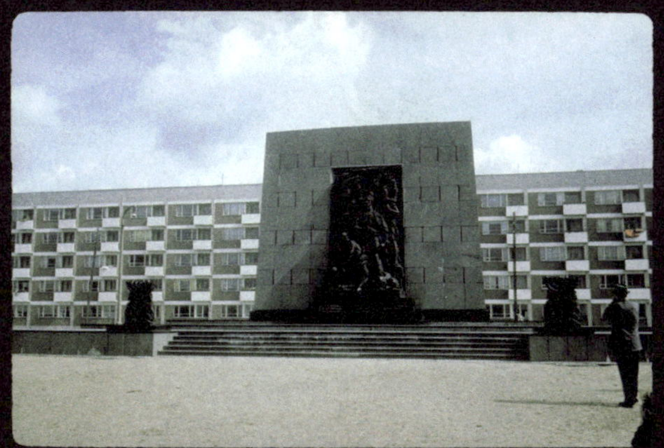

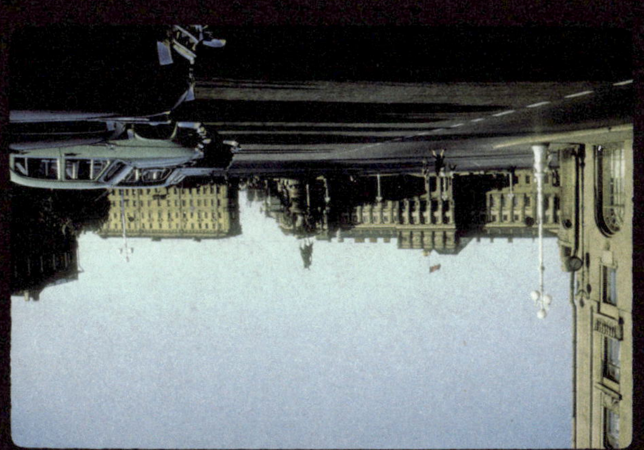

Lacuna Park

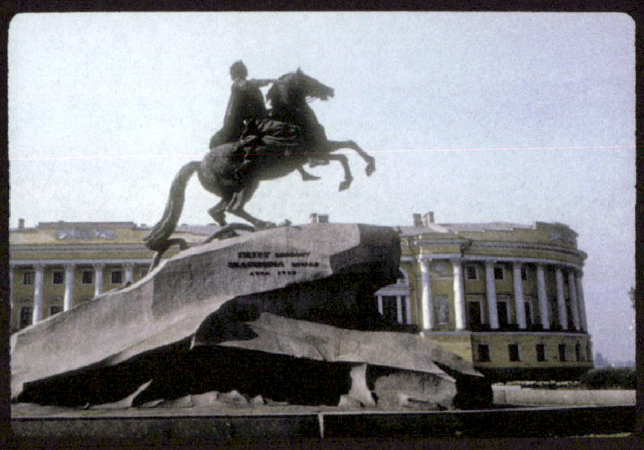

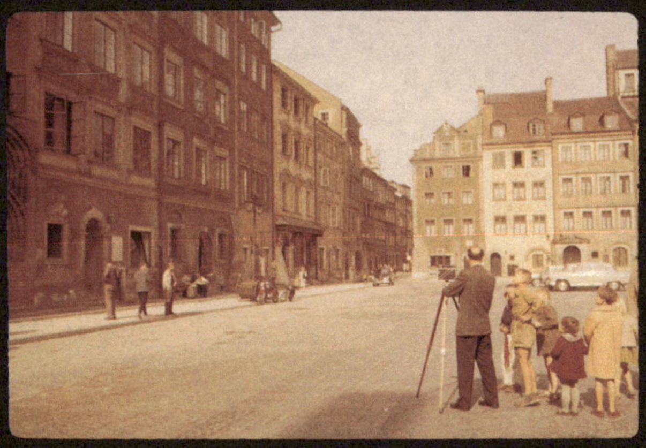

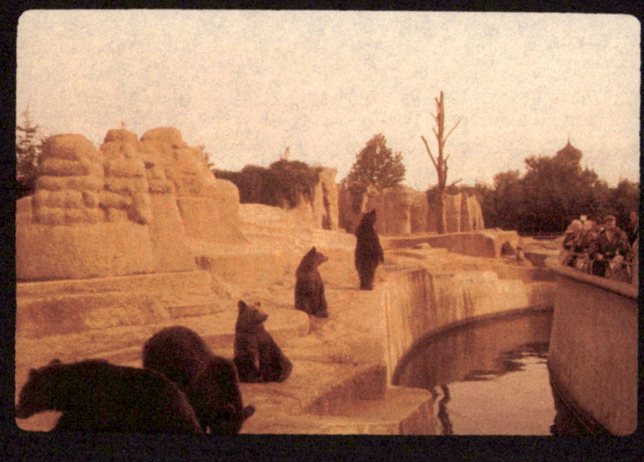

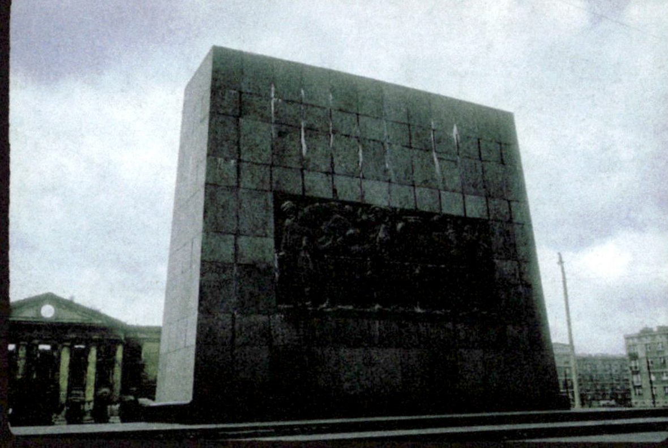

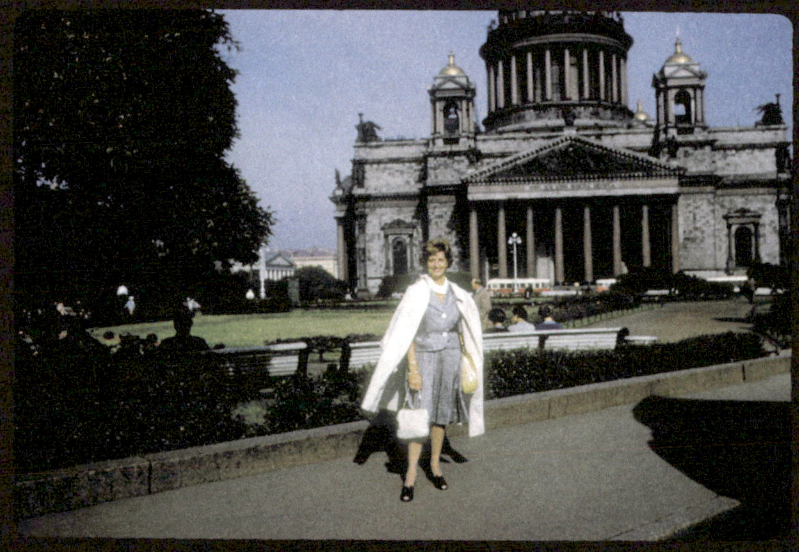

And sometimes, when the monument is not a thing but another, you are content to gamble on them. Looking at this photograph of my aunt, made by her husband, I am struck by the power of being and meaning that pervades her. Her foot steps forward in the frame. She outshines the gilt cathedral domes. She is Peter on horseback, Lenin with his overcoat flapping in the wind, a movie star after the premiere. And the photographer sees in her – we see, too – the accomplishment of the moment and the ideal in her advancing figure. Temporarily, we have stopped the racing, forgotten the subject's potential unwillingness or failure to carry it all. We see him seeing her and we yearn to believe that the structure is true. He has a monument that is his own; and he means something, too.

<u>Conclusions</u>

We tend to assume that when we look at a photograph, or a monument, we want it to mean something. But I'm not so sure. I think, often, that what we feel is that yearning towards being and meaning in which our subject is perpetually caught. We want to know the aliveness of the space between the learnable and the unknowable. We are brought into sympathy with that experience because it is also ours.

One more thing about my town: If you look at it on a map – for despite its absences, West Danby is always marked – you may register another point of geographical interest. The town is situated almost exactly halfway between the village of Candor to the southeast and the hamlet of Covert to the northwest. Thus, one may say, without taking liberties, that it resides at the reticent midpoint between disclosure and concealment. Here, again, the town is like a photograph.

Originally published as *The Photograph Commands Indifference* by Nicholas Muellner, (Ithaca, NY: A-Jump Books, 2009).

Image Credits

All images by Nicholas Muellner, except as follows:

Cover: Michael Robinson. Past the Mission, 2015. (detail)
              Courtesy the artist.

p. xi   Michael Robinson. Past the Mission, 2015.
              Courtesy the artist.

p. 2   Courtesy Lionel Monsky and Ada Muellner

p. 7   Courtesy Nikki Schiwal

p. 8   Nikki Schiwal, ca. 1990s.
              Courtesy the artist

p. 19   Superman II, film-still

p. 20   Superman II, film-still

p. 32   Caspar David Friedrich. *Night in a Harbour (Sisters)*.
              Between 1818 and 1820. Courtesy the Russian State
              Hermitage Museum.

p. 39   Mark Morrisroe, Untitled [John S. and Jonathan], 1985
              © The Estate of Mark Morrisroe (Ringier Collection) at
              Fotomuseum Winterthur

pp. 49-55   Ahndraya Parlato and Greg Halpern. Six photographs,
              all *Untitled* from *East of the Sun, West of the Moon*.
              Courtesy the artists.

pp. 75-85   Ron Jude. Six photographs, all *Untitled* from *Lick Creek Line*.
              Courtesy the artist.

p. 125   Lewis Carroll. *John Ruskin*, 1875.
              Courtesy the National Portrait Gallery.

p. 125   Paul Strand. *Alfred Stieglitz, Lake George, NY, 1929*.
              © Aperture Foundation, Inc., Paul Strand Archive

p. 126   Oscar Gustave Reijlander. *The Infant Photography Giving the
              Painter an Additional Brush*, c. 1856.
              Image courtesy the J. Paul Getty Museum.

p. 128   Anne Brigman, *Finis*, c. 1910. Stieglitz published this image in
              issue 48 of Camerawork, in 1912.

p. 129   Alfred Stieglitz, *Portrait of Georgia Engelhard*, 1922.
              Image courtesy the Museum of Modern Art.

p. 130   Gertrude Käsebier, *The Pathos of the Jackass*, c. 1900.
              Image courtesy the Library of Congress.

Colophon

Lacuna Park – Essays and Other Adventures in Photography
by Nicholas Muellner

Publisher: Bruno Ceschel
Editor: Tom Ridgway
Designer: Brian Paul Lamotte
Font: Graebenbach & Bembo
Printer: Grafiche Veneziane
Printed and bound in Italy

Acknowledgments

Across the span of a decade, a lucky man may accrue many debts. I'm particularly thankful to Bruno Ceschel for his wise and reckless vision, and to Ron Jude and Danielle Mericle of A-Jump Books for their foolhardy confidence, insight and support, as well as to others who commissioned or published some of these works, including Ahndraya Parlato and Greg Halpern, Agnieszka Piotrowska, Michael Mack, Shaan Tariq Hassan-Syed, Alexandra Muschovi and Karen vanMeenen.

Thanks to Brian Paul Lamotte for his brilliant design of this book; to my tenderly candid readers: Matthew Connors, Jason Livingston, Ada Muellner, Ahndraya Parlato, Helen Rubinstein and Catherine Taylor; to Gerry Beegan for his original layout of *The Photograph Commands Indifference*; to my dear Michael Robinson, who can see in the dark; and to my parents, who let me build an unventilated darkroom in a basement bedroom, and wash my prints in a bathtub.

This book is for Molly, Greta, Ronan, Ciaran, Adlai and Peata.
Your brilliance is a flashbulb lighting up the future.

Lacuna Park is made possible in part by a James B. Pendleton Grant from the Roy H. Park School of Communications at Ithaca College.

ISBN 978-1-9998144-8-9
First edition published in September 2019 by SPBH Editions

SPBH EDITIONS

SPBH Editions is the publishing house of Self Publish, Be Happy
Studio 2, 38-50 Pritchard's Rd, London E2 9AP, UK
selfpublishbehappy.com

Available through ARTBOOK | D.A.P.
75 Broad Street, Suite 630, New York, NY 10004, USA
www.artbook.com